OECD Public Governance Reviews

OECD Integrity Review of Thailand

TOWARDS COHERENT AND EFFECTIVE INTEGRITY POLICIES

Please cite this publication as:
OECD (2018), *OECD Integrity Review of Thailand: Towards Coherent and Effective Integrity Policies*, OECD Public Governance Reviews, OECD Publishing, Paris.
http://dx.doi.org/10.1787/9789264291928-en

ISBN 978-92-64-29191-1 (print)
ISBN 978-92-64-29192-8 (PDF)
ISBN 978-92-64-29193-5 (epub)

Series: OECD Public Governance Reviews
ISSN 2219-0406 (print)
ISSN 2219-0414 (online)

Photo credits: Cover ©lOvE lOvE/Shutterstock.com

Corrigenda to OECD publications may be found on line at: *www.oecd.org/about/publishing/corrigenda.htm.*

Foreword

The *OECD Integrity Review of Thailand* is the first of its kind in South East Asia, demonstrating the Government of Thailand's commitment to investing in public integrity and learning from the practices and expertise of OECD countries. The Review was conducted by the Directorate for Public Governance through a series of consultations with the Thai stakeholders, and is part of the Directorate's broader work programme on public sector integrity. Tackling corruption in the public sector and building transparent and accountable public institutions fosters investment, encourages competition, and improves government efficiency. The policy recommendations in this Integrity Review not only seek to bolster Thailand's integrity system, but also to promote public trust and ensure that the country can continue down a path of sustained economic growth.

In recent decades, the Government of Thailand has strengthened efforts to mitigate corruption risks in the public sector, as demonstrated by the establishment of agencies such as the National Anti-Corruption Commission (NACC), the Public Sector Anti-Corruption Commission (PACC), and the Office of the Auditor General. Furthermore, the third phase of the National Anti-Corruption Strategy (2017-21) seeks to deter corruption through stronger integrity and anti-corruption laws and policies. These developments have improved legal and institutional frameworks, but further progress is needed in some areas. This includes ensuring the effective implementation of integrity laws and policies which would lead to improvements in the levels of public trust.

This Integrity Review analyses Thailand's integrity system, including the institutional framework for its anti-corruption strategy, conflict-of-interest policies, ethics management in the public sector and whistleblower protection. It provides recommendations in line with international good practices and the 2017 *OECD Recommendation on Public Integrity*.

The Review suggests a streamlined mechanism for co-ordinating among bodies, in particular the NACC, PACC and the Office of the Civil Service Commission (OCSC). The government could develop more detailed guidance for officials considered at risk of conflict-of-interest situations, and further expand the scope of its asset declaration system to public officials that are considered at risk of corruption. At the same time, it should consider developing an online disclosure system to facilitate the submission, verification and audit, and subsequent publication of asset declarations.

To foster a culture of public integrity, Thailand could increase awareness of the Code of Professional Ethics for Civil Servants by developing an in-depth training programme, and introduce a dedicated whistleblower protection law to facilitate reporting of suspected integrity violations.

Marcos Bonturi
OECD Director for Public Governance

Acknowledgements

Under the direction and oversight of Marcos Bonturi, Director for Public Governance, and János Bertók, Head of the Public Sector Integrity Division, this review was coordinated by Yukihiko Hamada and Jeroen Michels, with the valuable guidance of Julio Bacio Terracino. The chapters were written by Jeroen Michels, Yukihiko Hamada and Lisa Kilduff.

The review was prepared for publication by Meral Gedik and Thibaut Gigou. Editorial assistance was provided by Andrea Uhrhammer and Victoria Elliot. Anaisa Goncalves and Pauline Alexandrov provided administrative assistance.

The OECD expresses its gratitude to the Government of Thailand, and in particular, to the Office of Public Sector Development Commission (OPDC) and the Public Sector Anti-Corruption Commission (PACC) for their support and inputs throughout the project. This review also significantly benefited from the comments provided by the National Anti-Corruption Commission (NACC) and the Office of the Civil Service Commission (OCSC). Particular appreciation goes to all the participants who actively engaged in debates and provided valuable insights during the fact finding mission in Bangkok on 21 - 25 November 2016. This review also benefitted from the valuable input of the officials from OPDC and PACC during their time at the OECD on the secondment programme in 2016 and 2017.

The OECD wishes to thank the German International Cooperation Agency (GIZ) for its financial support.

Table of contents

Tables

Figures

Boxes

Acronyms and abbreviations

ACOC	Anti-Corruption Operation Centres
AMLA	Anti-Money Laundering Act
ASEAN	Association of South East Asian Nations
B.E.	Buddhist Era
BMA	Bangkok Metropolitan Administration
BoB	Bureau of Budget
CAN	High-Level Anti-Corruption Commission of Peru
CSO	Civil society organisations
DC	District of Columbia
EUR	Euro
GBP	Pound sterling
GDP	Gross domestic product
HDI	Human Development Index
HRM	Human resources management
IPI	Index of Public Integrity
ITA	Integrity and Transparency Assessment
JPY	Japanese yen
KNAB	Corruption Prevention and Combating Bureau of Latvia
KPK	Corruption Eradication Commission of Indonesia
KRW	Korean won
MP	Member of Parliament
NACC	National Anti-Corruption Commission
NCCFC	National Citizens' Committee for the Fight against Corruption
NCM	National Committee for Moralisation of Colombia
NCPO	National Council for Peace and Order
NESDB	National Economic and Social Development Board
NGO	Non-governmental organisation
NHS	National Health Service of the United Kingdom

OCSC	Office of the Civil Service Commission
ONSC	Office of the National Security Council
OPDC	Office of the Public Sector Development Commission
PACC	Public Sector Anti-Corruption Commission
PID Act	Australia's Public Interest Disclosure Act
PSDPA	Canada's Public Servants Disclosure Protection Act
THB	Thai baht
UNCAC	United Nations Convention Against Corruption
UNDP	United Nations Development Program
UNODC	United Nations Office on Drugs and Crime

Executive summary

Anti-corruption laws in Thailand have been expanded over time and the current National Anti-Corruption Strategy includes bold efforts to mitigate corruption risks. To support the Government of Thailand's commitment to public integrity, the OECD *Integrity Review of Thailand* provides in-depth analysis of the country's public integrity system. In line with the 2017 *OECD Recommendation on Public Integrity*, the Review offers guidance on how to strengthen Thailand's integrity frameworks and policies, based on good practices from OECD countries.

Towards co-ordinated integrity institutions

Although Thailand has an extensive legislative framework in place for public integrity, the mandates of various institutions overlap, reducing the effectiveness of anti-corruption and integrity policies and hindering their implementation. For instance, the National Anti-Corruption Commission (NACC) and the Public Sector Anti-Corruption Commission (PACC) have conflicting responsibilities in relation to developing and implementing integrity policies. Furthermore, multiple bodies are currently responsible for investigating cases of corruption, weakening the investigative process. This overlap could be addressed by building on the mandate of the NACC for the overall co-ordination of anti-corruption and integrity policies, and on the specialised role of the PACC in preventing corruption in the executive branch. A clear co-ordination mechanism among these bodies, as well as others such as the Office of the Civil Service Commission, would allow integrity and anti-corruption policies to be developed and implemented more consistently.

Thailand has broad guiding principles for managing conflict of interest in the public sector as well as practical guidelines to assist public officials in identifying and preventing conflict-of-interest situations. However, there are positions in the public sector that are considered more at risk from conflict of interest and integrity violations, such as procurement and custom officials. An increasing number of OECD countries have developed specific, detailed guidance for such individuals, enabling them to better manage potential conflicts of interest. Thailand could look at these experiences and consider further developing the guidance for public officials that are susceptible to conflict-of-interest situations. The PACC, with its preventative mandate, would be the ideal body to develop such guidance in the executive branch.

A robust asset disclosure system is an effective tool for ensuring the accountability of public officials and facilitating the detection of illicit activity. In Thailand, the NACC expanded the scope of the provisions for asset disclosure to include senior political positions. While this is a positive development, Thailand's asset disclosure system could be further broadened to include senior civils servants and at-risk officials in order to mitigate conflict of interest risks. This could be complemented by strengthening the auditing capacity of NACC with an online system to facilitate submission, effective auditing and verification, and subsequent publication by NACC.

Cultivating a culture of integrity

To promote a culture of integrity in the public sector, all public officials are expected to understand the public sector values underpinning their role as well as how to apply them in daily operations. In the Thai public sector, the Code of Professional Ethics for Civil Servants is known to employees, but a comprehensive training programme would help civil servants apply the Code in fulfilling their duties. PACC could carry out such training for civil servants and institutional partners, and provide guidance and support on integrity issues in the executive branch. Awareness-raising activities could also be extended to include the broader public and promote a whole-of-society approach to anti-corruption, enhancing public trust in Thai institutions.

To foster an open organisational culture and allow for detection of integrity violations, individuals must feel that they can raise concerns freely and without fear of reprisal. In Thailand, some protection is afforded under witness protection and related laws, but the provisions do not go far enough. In line with an increasing number of OECD countries, Thailand could consider adopting a dedicated whistleblower protection law that offers comprehensive protection measures to assure public officials that they can report suspected wrongdoing without constraint. In particular, such legislation is expected to clearly identify the scope of whistleblowers, stipulate the reporting channels available to employees, and define prohibited forms of retaliation. Furthermore, OECD good practices show that such measures are more effective when accompanied by awareness-raising activities to ensure that individuals have a clear idea of how to make a disclosure, and what protection is afforded to them when doing so. Once a dedicated whistleblower protection law is in place, PACC could be the agency in charge of overseeing its implementation and training public officials in the executive branch.

Chapter 1. An overview of governance and corruption in Thailand

This chapter assesses the current situation in Thailand with regards to governance and corruption. Looking at international indicators as well as the perspectives on corruption of both business and citizens in Thailand, the analysis shows that corruption and bribery are prevalent in both the public and the private sectors. These results highlight the need for Thailand to strengthen its governance framework and promote a culture of integrity to mitigate corruption risks.

Introduction

Corruption perpetuates inequality and poverty, negatively affecting the well-being of citizens. It can result in the unequal distribution of income and undermine opportunities for individuals to participate in social, economic and political life (OECD, 2017[1]). Corruption also hampers a country's economic development. Indeed, it has a negative impact on investment, competition, human capital formation and government efficiency. Erosion of public trust and widening socio-economic inequalities are exacerbated by corruption in the public sector. It is therefore imperative that governance systems contain strong mechanisms to mitigate the risks of corruption and to ensure the effective delivery of public services.

Integrity is essential for building strong institutions, and assures citizens that the government is working in their interest. Strengthening public integrity means shifting from *ad hoc* anti-corruption and integrity policies to a comprehensive, risk-based approach, with an emphasis on cultivating a culture of integrity across the whole of government and society. A sound governance system is needed to control corruption and provide a stable environment.

Thailand has benefited from socioeconomic development and improved well-being in the past 25 years, making significant gains in reducing poverty and inequality. The country's Human Development Index (HDI) increased by 28.9% from 0.57 to 0.74 between 1990 and 2015, a figure that is slightly above the average of the Association of Southeast Asian Nations (ASEAN) countries (Figure 1.1). In the same period, the country experienced fluctuations in economic growth during extended periods of social and political turmoil (Figure 1.2).

Figure 1.1. Human Development Index (2015)

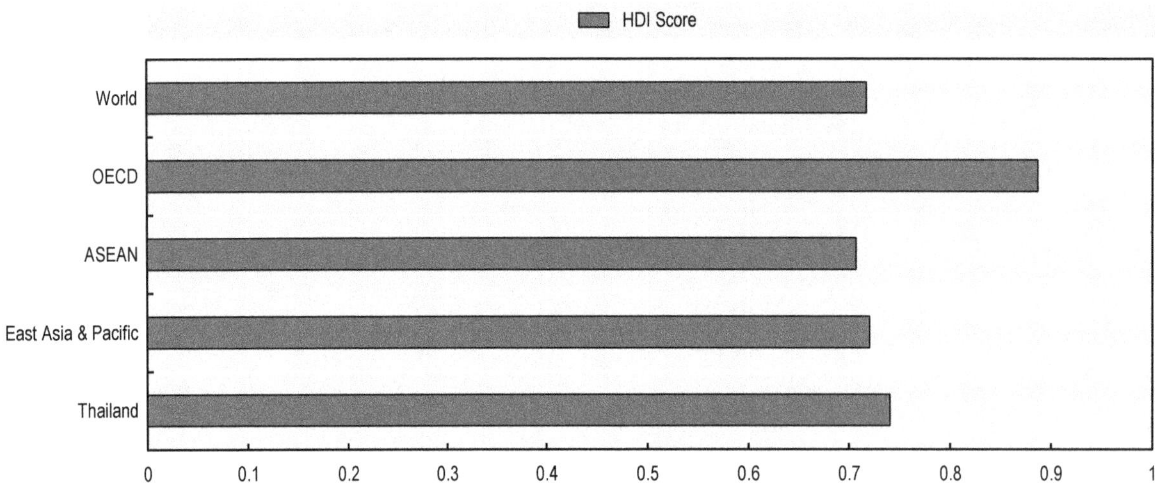

Source: (UNDP,(n.d.)[2])

Figure 1.2. Thailand's growth in gross domestic product (GDP) per capita

Source: (The World Bank, 2017[3]).

To control corruption effectively and maintain trust in public institutions, a sound governance system must be in place. In Thailand, military state control of politics, interspersed with short periods of democracy, has characterised much of the country's recent history. The current military government, the National Council for Peace and Order (NCPO) has sustained economic stability since it took power in 2014.

International governance and corruption indicators

Perception of corruption in Thailand remains significantly high. Thailand is perceived to be less corrupt than some of its neighbours, and is on an equal footing with the Philippines, but overall, its score is below the average of ASEAN countries (Figure 1.3). With regards to the components of the World Bank's World Governance Indicators, Thailand is below the average of ASEAN and OECD countries (Figure 1.4). In the Index of Public Integrity (IPI) 2016, Thailand scores lower than the average of OECD countries that are included in the index, but performs better within the regional perspective (Figure 1.5).

Figure 1.3. Thailand's Corruption Perception Index, in comparison with that of ASEAN and OECD countries

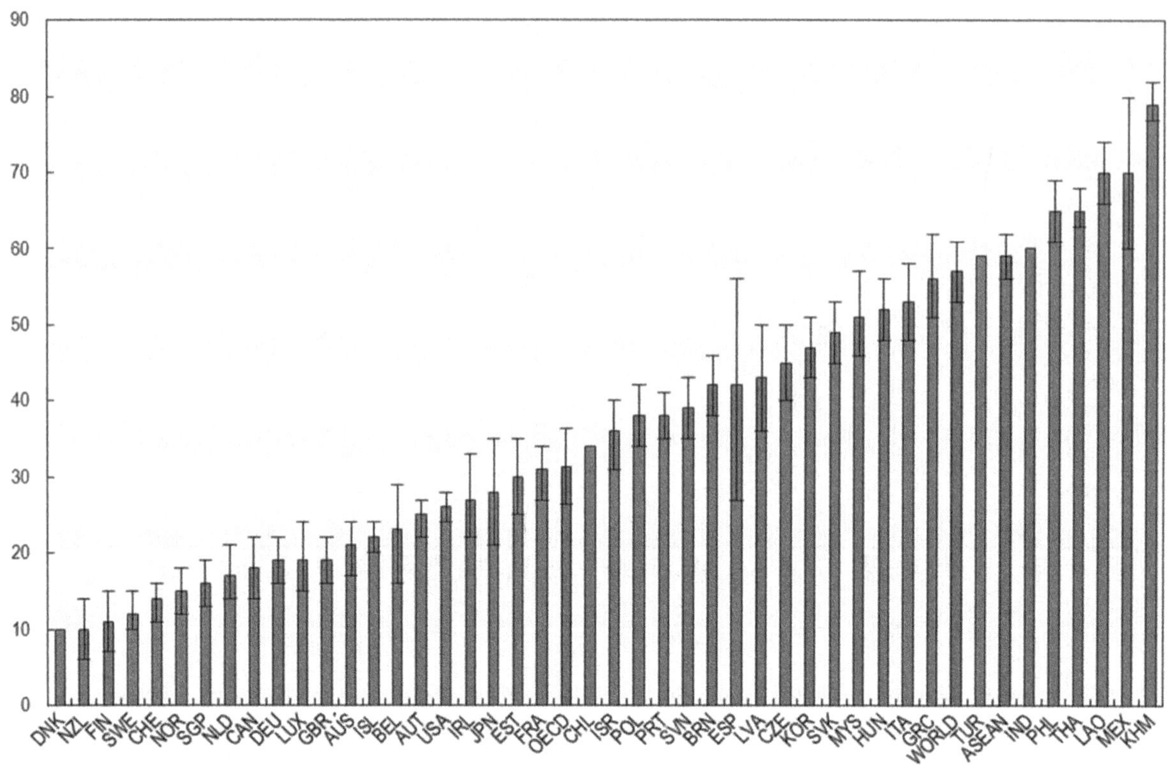

Note: Vietnam is not represented, since the relevant data was not available.
Source: (Transparency International, 2016[4])

Figure 1.4. World Governance Indicators 2016

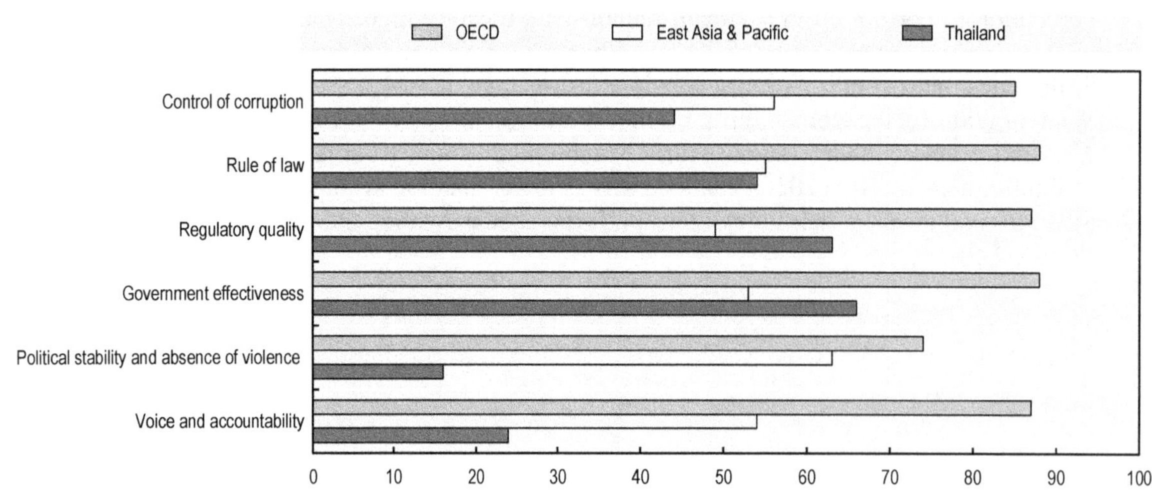

Source: (The World Bank, 2016[5])

Figure 1.5. Index of Public Integrity (IPI) 2016

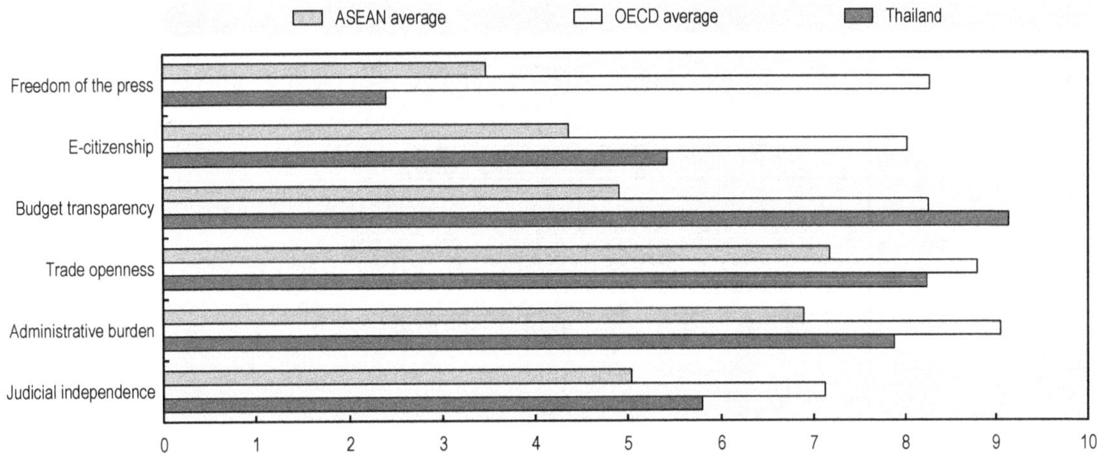

Note: The IPI aims to address a country's capacity to control corruption based on composite scores in six sub-components: Freedom of the press, e-citizenship, budget transparency, trade openness, administrative burden and judicial independence. ASEAN countries covered are: Cambodia, Indonesia, Malaysia, Myanmar, Philippines, Thailand and Vietnam. All OECD countries are included except Australia, Canada, Iceland, Israel, Japan and Switzerland.
Source: (European Research Centre for Anti-Corruption and State-Building, 2016[6])

The business perspective on corruption

In the World Economic Forum's Global Competitiveness Report 2016-2017, corruption is cited as the third biggest obstacle to doing business in Thailand, exceeded only by "government instability" and "inefficient government bureaucracy" (Figure 1.6).

Some of these factors are interrelated; indeed, when government bureaucracies are not fit for purpose, there are more opportunities for officials to engage in rent-seeking behaviour, such as extracting bribes. Government instability and the fourth most important problem listed, "policy instability", may also mean that entrepreneurs looking to do business in Thailand may have to interact with an uncertain bureaucratic environment that is more susceptible to corruption.

In the World Bank's Enterprise Surveys, Thailand displays lower scores in areas related to gift-giving aimed at securing contracts or obtaining permits, but performs better in comparison to the rest of the region (Figure 1.7).

Figure 1.6. Perceived obstacles to doing business in Thailand from the Global Competitiveness Report 2016-17

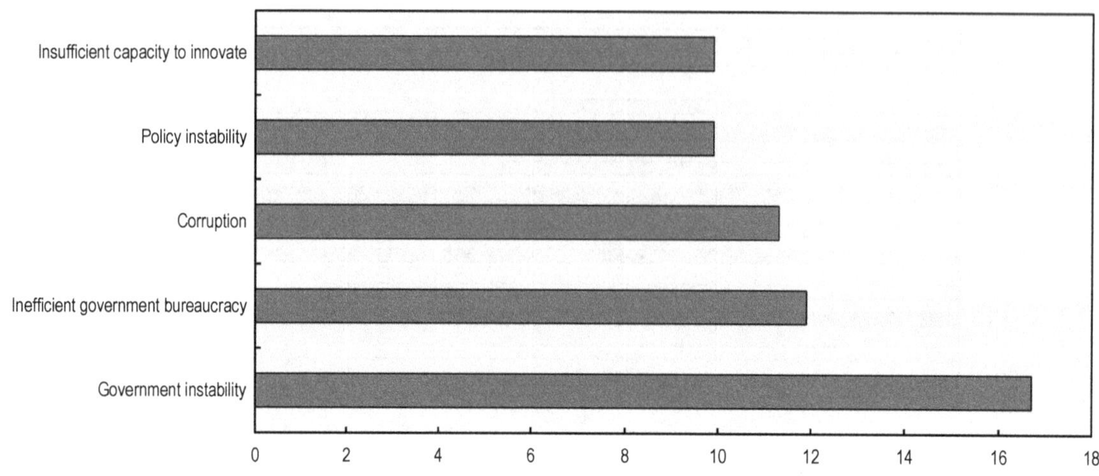

Source: (World Economic Forum, 2017[7])

Figure 1.7. World Enterprise Surveys 2016

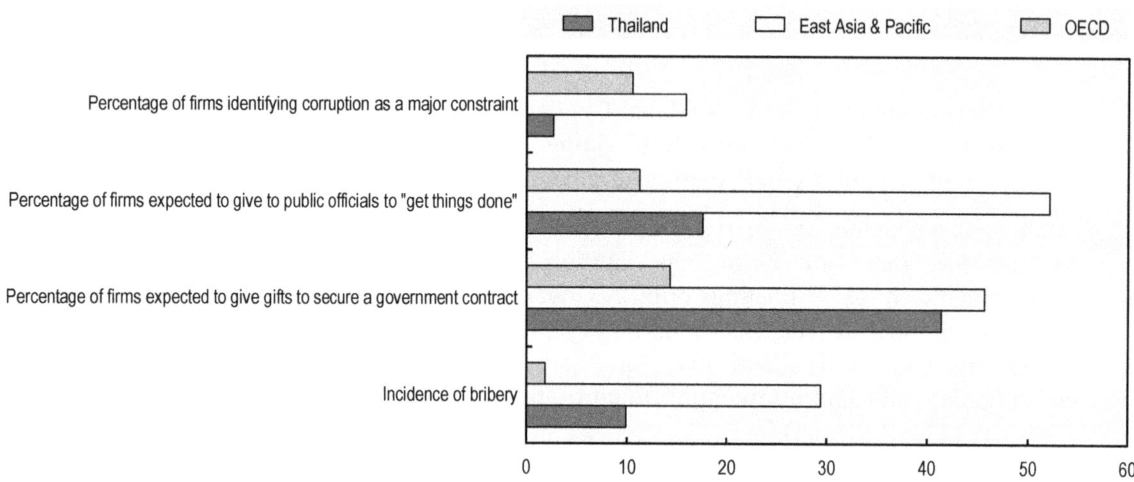

Source: (World Bank Group, 2016[8])

The citizen perspective on corruption

A report of the Global Corruption Barometer 2017 in the Asia Pacific region reveals that only 14% of people surveyed in Thailand believed that corruption had increased over the last year, the lowest percentage in the region (Figure 1.8).

There was also a positive response to government efforts, with 72% of respondents saying that the government is doing well in fighting corruption. Nevertheless, some serious problems persist at the institutional level: 78% of respondents consider the police to be highly corrupt, and 41% reported having to pay a bribe, give a gift or do a favour for somebody when accessing public services.

Figure 1.8. Percentage of respondents who believe that corruption has increased in Asia Pacific countries

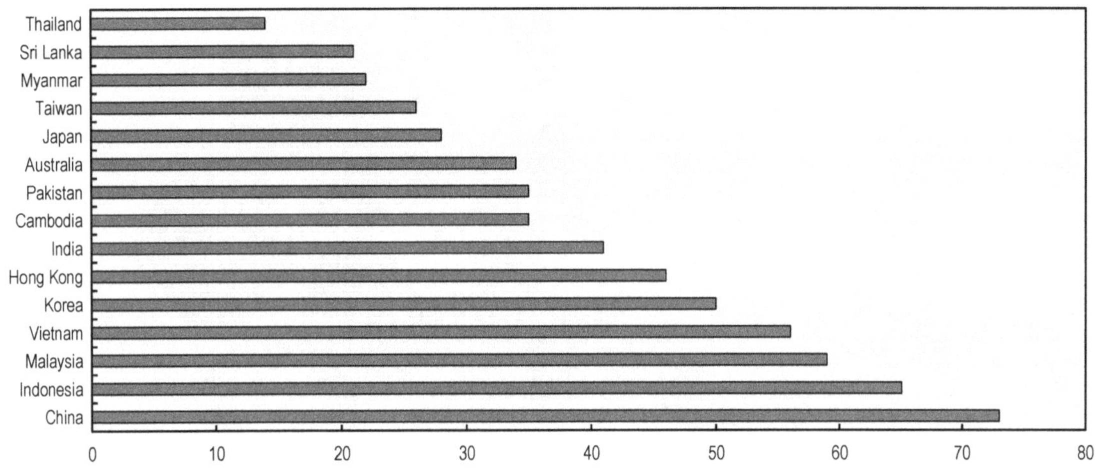

Source: (Transparency International, 2017[9])

The review's analytical framework for assessing public sector integrity

The previous section provides insight into how Thailand is affected by corruption in both the public and private sector, and underscores the need to strengthen anti-corruption and integrity policies to reinforce the country's integrity system. With a view to supporting the Government of Thailand in this process and providing recommendations for ongoing reform, the OECD Integrity Review assesses the strengths and weaknesses of Thailand's policies for public sector integrity (i.e. integrity practices for the public administration). In line with the recently approved OECD Recommendation of the Council on Public Integrity (Figure 1.9), the review specifically examines key dimensions of Thailand's public integrity system and its implementation, including:

- The coherence and comprehensiveness of the public integrity system: Chapter 2 describes the institutional architecture created by the national anti-corruption system, and how adequately it covers the key elements of strong public integrity systems. Recommended improvements for policies concerning public ethics are discussed in Chapter 3, while Chapter 4 analyses how effectively the Government of Thailand manages conflict-of-interest and asset declarations. The extent to which Thailand's integrity policies cultivate a culture of integrity is evaluated, specifically by: i) promoting a whole-of-society approach to fighting corruption;

ii) investing in integrity leadership; iii) promoting a merit-based professional public service; iv) providing information, training, guidance and advice for public officials; and v) supporting open organisational cultures responsive to public integrity concerns. Chapters 2 and 3, for instance, will examine the extent to which government institutions engage with non-governmental stakeholders in the fight against corruption. They also touch upon the linkages of integrity policies with human resources management practices (particularly recruitment, performance assessment, capacity building and training). Chapter 5 discusses how whistleblower protection and reporting mechanisms can contribute to an organisational culture that supports integrity standards.

Figure 1.9. 2017 OECD Recommendation on Public Integrity, showing the analytical framework for the integrity review

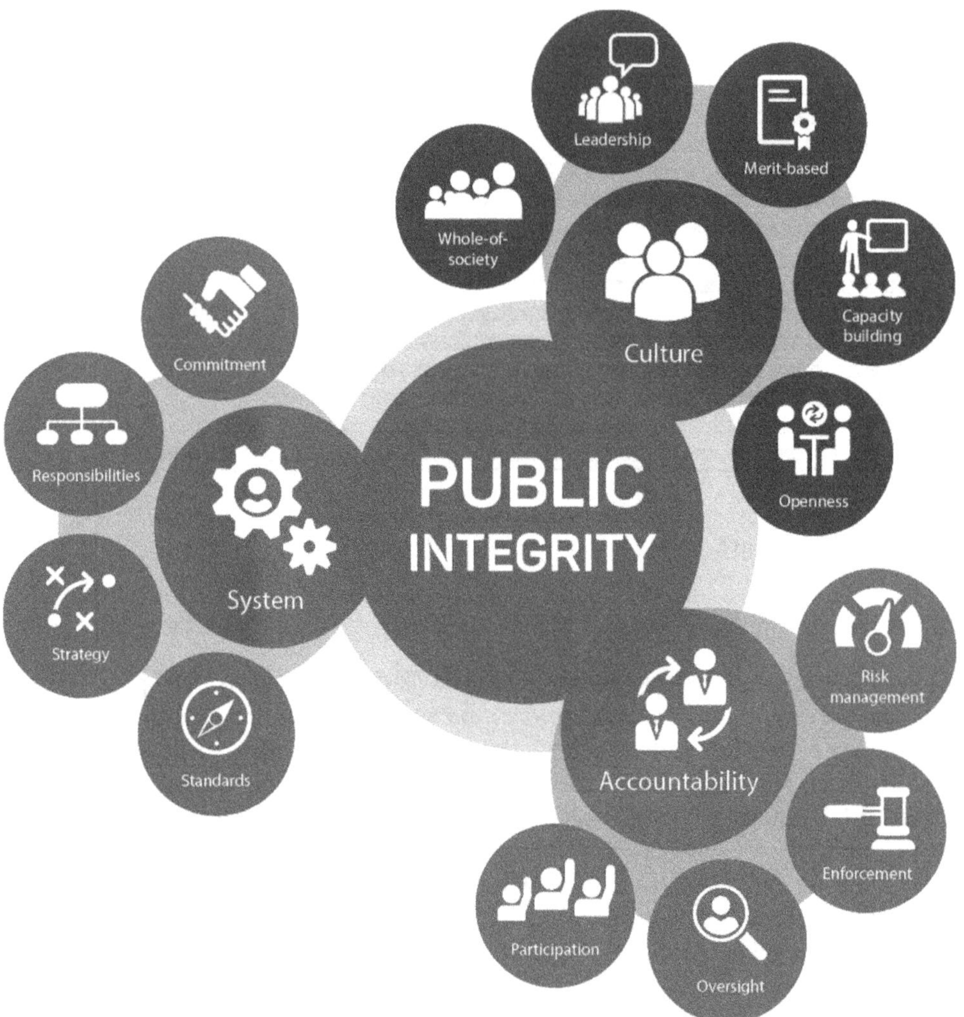

Source: (OECD, 2017[1])

References

European Research Centre for Anti-Corruption and State-Building (2016), *Index of Public Integrity*, http://integrity-index.org/. [6]

OECD (2017), *OECD Recommendation of the Council on Public Integrity*, http://www.oecd.org/gov/ethics/Recommendation-Public-Integrity.pdf. [1]

The World Bank (2016), *The World Bank Group World Governance Indicators*, http://info.worldbank.org/governance/wgi/#reports. [5]

The World Bank (2017), *The World Bank Group World Development Indicators*, https://data.worldbank.org/indicator/NY.GDP.MKTP.KD.ZG?end=2015&locations=TH&start=1990 (accessed on 26 January 2018). [3]

Transparency International (2016), *Corruption Perceptions Index*, https://www.transparency.org/news/feature/corruption_perceptions_index_2016. [4]

Transparency International (2017), *Transparency International Asia Pacific Corruption Barometer*, https://www.transparency.org/whatwedo/publication/people_and_corruption_asia_pacific_global_corruption_barometer. [9]

UNDP((n.d.)), *Human Development Index (HDI)*, http://hdr.undp.org/en/content/human-development-index-hdi (accessed on 26 January 2018). [2]

World Bank Group (2016), *World Enterprise Surveys*, http://www.enterprisesurveys.org/. [8]

World Economic Forum (2017), *The Global Competitiveness Report 2016–2017*, https://www.weforum.org/reports/the-global-competitiveness-report-2016-2017-1 (accessed on 26 January 2018). [7]

Chapter 2. Encouraging a comprehensive and co-ordinated integrity system in Thailand

This chapter examines the institutional arrangements for public integrity established in Thailand at the central level against the principles of the OECD 2017 Recommendation on Public Integrity. Thailand is advised to strengthen the development, implementation and monitoring of the National Anti-Corruption Strategy and integrate the Integrity and Transparency Assessment in the Strategy. Thailand may also improve institutional co-ordination by streamlining the mandates of the National Anti-Corruption Commission (NACC), the Public Sector Anti-Corruption Commission (PACC) and the Office of the Civil Service Commission (OCSC), and encourage mainstreaming of anti-corruption policies by strengthening the capacity of Anti-Corruption Operation Centres (ACOCs). Thailand is also advised to strengthen stakeholder consultation and knowledge management in the field of public integrity.

Introduction: Effective public integrity systems

Corruption and lack of integrity in public decision-making undermine the values of democracy and trust in governments, impede the effective delivery of public services, and are a threat to inclusive growth. While cases of corruption need to be investigated and sanctioned, in-depth preventive actions are necessary to address systemic and institutional weaknesses that facilitate corruption in the first place. Put differently, countries face the challenge of moving from a reactive "culture of cases" to a proactive "culture of integrity".

A preventive approach to corruption requires a coherent and effective public integrity system, given the complexity and wide variety of integrity breaches and corrupt practices. Managing public integrity is not only the responsibility of specialised anti-corruption bodies, but the responsibility of all organisations within the public sector. The private sector, civil society and citizens also share responsibility for tackling corruption and ensuring integrity.

Country practices show that an effective public integrity system requires demonstrating commitment at the highest political and management levels of the public sector, and clarifying institutional responsibilities at the relevant levels (organisational, subnational or national, and within the different sectors) for designing, leading and implementing the elements of the integrity system. It is also necessary to ensure appropriate mandates and capacities to fulfil these responsibilities. Since the promotion of integrity involves many different actors, mechanisms for co-operation between the actors, sectors and subnational levels have to be in place to avoid fragmentation, overlap and gaps, to support coherence, and to share and build on lessons learned from good practices. Clear, comprehensive, and effective arrangements are of the utmost importance in ensuring the impact of integrity policies. Weaknesses in this co-ordination may considerably diminish the effectiveness of anti-corruption efforts, and even generate loopholes that allow corrupt actors to escape prosecution.

In Thailand, the government has declared anti-corruption efforts an urgent issue and part of the national agenda. Prime Minister General Prayut Chan-o-cha has on several occasions emphasised the need to include anti-corruption efforts in the reform process of every sector, whether in politics, the economy, energy, public health and the environment, mass media, social affairs or on other issues (The Nation, 2016[1]).

Thailand's anti-corruption laws offer an extensive legislative framework for anti-corruption. Offences of this nature are captured primarily in the Organic Act, the Penal Code, the Offences Relating to the Submission of Bids to State Agencies Act and the Organic Act on Counter Corruption, B.E. 2542 (1999). The Organic Act on Counter Corruption criminalises corrupt practices of public officials, except for the acceptance of benefits "on an ethical basis" in accordance with the NACC Supplemental Rules. Moreover, the Organic Act on Counter Corruption, B.E. 2542 (1999), and its amendment (No. 3), B.E. 2558 (2015), Section 123/5, stipulate the liability of legal persons involved in the bribery of public officials, foreign public officials and officials of international organisations. Under Thai law, a person involved in bribery holds "corporate liability". This stipulation complies with the United Nations Convention Against Corruption (UNCAC) and the OECD Convention on Combating Bribery of Foreign Public Officials in International Business Transactions. The Thai Penal Code criminalises active and passive bribery of public officials by persons operating in the public or private sector. The Act on Offences Relating to the Submission of Bids to State Agencies defines corrupt practices in relation to public procurement, such as bid collusion. The Anti-Money Laundering Act (AMLA) prohibits money laundering and is implemented by the Anti-Money Laundering Office. Finally, Thailand is a State Party to the United Nations Convention Against Corruption (UNCAC), but not the OECD Anti-Bribery Convention.

As much as anti-corruption efforts are a duty of all government institutions, various government actors play a leading role in preventing, investigating and sanctioning corruption while enhancing integrity. As in most countries, Thailand has various public institutions directly or indirectly involved in either corruption prevention or detection, or both. For corruption prevention in the public sector at the national level, an overview of key actors leading anti-corruption efforts can be found in Table 2.1.

Table 2.1. Key government actors in the public integrity system in Thailand

National Anti-Corruption Commission (NACC)	Constitutionally independent commission	Independent anti-corruption agency with a preventive mandate for all sectors and an investigative mandate for high-ranking officials Lead agency for the National Anti-Corruption Strategy Lead agency for the strategic-Integrated budget for anti-corruption	Constitution, B.E. 2560 (2017), of the Thailand Organic Act on Counter Corruption, B.E. 2542 (1999), amended in B.E.2554 (2011), The Act on Offences Relating to the Submission of Bids to Government Agencies, B.E. 2542 (1999) and B.E. 2558 (2015), and the Act on Offences Committed by Officials of State Organisations or Agencies, B.E. 2502 (1959)
Public Sector Anti-Corruption Commission (PACC)	Government agency part of the executive branch, reporting to the Prime Minister	Promotion of integrity of public officials Investigation of cases involving low-ranking public servants Implementation of the Integrity and Transparency Assessment (ITA) Co-ordination of Anti-Corruption Operation Centres	Executive Measures in Anti-Corruption Act, B.E. 2551 (2008), and No. 2, B.E. 2559 (2016), NCPO Order No.69/2557, dated 18 June 18 2014
Office of the Public Sector Development Commission (OPDC)	Government agency reporting to the Prime Minister	Criteria and Procedures for Good Governance, including public participation and transparency Institutional arrangements within the public administration	Public Administration Act, B.E.2545 (2002), Royal Decree on Criteria and Procedures for Good Governance, B.E. 2546 (2003), Licensing Facilitation Act, B.E. 2558 (2015)
Office of the Civil Service Commission (OCSC)	Government agency reporting to the Prime Minister	Central agency for human resource (HR) standards, including civil service ethics, disciplinary regime, complaint handling, Code of Conduct for civil servants	Civil Service Act, B.E.2551 (2008)

Source: Government of Thailand.

The following interlinked recommendations are proposed, related i) to the development, implementation and monitoring of the National Anti-Corruption Strategy, and ii) to institutional co-ordination and stakeholder engagement:

Development, implementation and monitoring of the National Anti-Corruption Strategy

In terms of policy instruments, the National Anti-Corruption Strategy is the main government guiding document in the area of anti-corruption and integrity. The Government Cabinet, in a meeting on 11 October 2016, approved the draft National Anti-Corruption Strategy, Phase 3, proposed by the Office of the National Anti-

Corruption Commission. The vision of the National Anti-Corruption Strategy is “Zero Tolerance and Clean Thailand”, which aims to achieve “a society founded on discipline, integrity and ethics, with all sectors participating in the prevention and suppression of corruption.”

The Third Phase of the National Anti-Corruption Strategy will be implemented from 2017 to 2021 and comprises both corruption prevention and law enforcement. The six aims of the National Anti-Corruption Strategy, Phase 3, are the following:

1. To create a society that does not tolerate corruption;
2. To promote political will to fight corruption;
3. To deter corruption in public policy;
4. To develop a proactive anti-corruption system;
5. To reform corruption suppression mechanisms and processes;
6. To improve Thailand’s Corruption Perception Index score.

In promoting the National Anti-Corruption Strategy, the Thai government also urges all agencies and institutions to undertake action against corruption, underscoring the whole-of-government approach to promote integrity and fight corruption. All government agencies and institutions are expected to adopt guidelines and measures in accordance with this strategy and to translate them into practice. Moreover, government bodies are instructed to include these actions and measures in their four-year State Administration Plans and their annual action plans. They are also instructed to start the implementation of the National Anti-Corruption Strategy, Phase 3, in the 2017 fiscal year onwards.

Moreover, in addition to the National Anti-Corruption Strategy, good governance and anti-corruption feature high on the political agenda in Thailand and are widely recognised as priorities. Good governance and anti-corruption feature in a large number of plans and strategies developed and/or supported by the Thai government, such as the 20 Years Country Strategy 2017-2036, the 12th National Economic and Social Development Plan 2017-2020, budget plans, and the 2030 Sustainable Development agenda (Figure 2.1).

Figure 2.1. Anti-corruption and good governance in national strategies and plans in Thailand

Mapping Different Strategies/ Plans

20 Years Country Strategy 2017-2036	12th National Economic and Social Development Plan (2017-2020)	Sustainable Development Goals (SDGs)	Budget Allocation Strategy for Fiscal Year 2017 (1 Oct 2016 - 30 Sep 2017)	25 Strategic-integrated Budget Plans (Fiscal Year 2017)	Government Policy *General Prayut Chan-o-cha, Prime Minister*
1. National Security	1. Strengthening and develop human capital capacity	1. No poverty	1. National Security	1. Building reconciliation and harmony within the society	Policy 1: Protection of Monarchy
2. Building Country's Competitiveness	2. Building fairness and reduce inequity in society	2. Zero hunger	2. Building Country's Competitiveness	2. Mobilizing problem solving in southern border provinces	Policy 2: Maintenance of state security and foreign affairs
3. Human Resource Development and Capacity Building	3. Strengthening a sustainable economic competitiveness	3. Good health and well-being	3. Human Resource Development and Capacity Building	3. Management of migrants and human trafficking	Policy 3: Reduction of social inequalities and building of opportunities and access to public services
4. Creating Social Opportunity and Equity	4. Environmental-friendly growth for sustainable development	4. Quality education	4. Reducing poverty, inequality, and create internal growth	4. Prevention, suppression, and rehabilitation drug addicts	Policy 4: Education and Learning
5. Growth with Environmental friendly and Quality of life	5. Strengthening national security for wealth and Sustainability	5. Gender equality	5. Water management and creating growth with Environmental friendly and Quality of life	5. Potential industry development	Policy 5: Upgrade of public health services and people's healthcare
6. Rebalancing and Developing Public Sector Administration	*6. Public administration, anti-corruption, and good governance*	6. Clean water and sanitation	*6. Rebalancing and Developing Public Sector Administration*	6. SMEs promotion	Policy 6: Enhancement of Economic Performance
	7. Developing infrastructure and logistics	7. Affordable and clean energy		7. Special Economic Zone development	Policy 7: Roles and Opportunities in ASEAN Community
	8. Science, technology, research and innovation development	8. Decent work and economic growth		8. Infrastructure and logistics development	Policy 8: Science and Technology, R&D, and Innovation
	9. Political and special economic zone development	9. Industry, innovation and infrastructure		9. Digital economy development	Policy 9: Maintenance of natural resources security and balance between conservation and sustainable utilization
	10. International cooperation for development	10. Reduce inequalities		10. Research and development promotion	*Policy 10: Promotion of good governance in state administration, and anti-corruption*
		11. Sustainable cities and communities		11. Generating income from tourism and services	
		12. Responsible consumption and production		12. Potential human development by age	
		13. Climate action		13. Raising quality of education and life-long learning	
		14. Life below water		14. Developing economic foundation and strong communities	
		15. Life on land		15. Arable land issues management	
		16. Peace, justice and strong institutions		16. Health insurance system development	
		17. Partnerships for the goals		17. Creating equality for aging society	
		16.5 Substantially reduce corruption and bribery in all their forms		18. Waste and environmental management	
				19. Developing and increasing efficiency in energy friendly utilization	
				20. Water resource management	
				21. Corruption and misconduct prevention and suppression	
				22. Legislation reform and justice development process	
				23. Ease of doing business	
				24. Promotion of decentralization to local administration	
				25. Promotion of integrated provincial and provincial cluster development	

Thailand could reinforce the National Anti-Corruption Strategy by expanding the secretariat function of the NACC Sub-Commission for Strategy Implementation

In developing the National Anti-Corruption Strategy, Phase 3, the designated NACC Working Group employed a consultative approach and collected the views and suggestions of experts, academics and representatives of government agencies, state enterprises, the private sector, non-governmental organisations (NGOs) and independent organisations, to obtain the widest possible coverage. Additionally, the working group invited the general public to submit their views at organised forums. The results of these forums were submitted to the working group and used as data for drafting the National Anti-Corruption Strategy.

In implementing the National Anti-Corruption Strategy, the NACC Sub-Commission for Strategy Implementation plays a pivotal role in co-ordinating with the various partners inside and outside the government. The sub-commission has developed a manual to provide guidance on implementation of the Strategy. However, the multi-stakeholder approach is not as well defined, and various institutional partners reported that their roles and expected contributions are not sufficiently spelled out. Moreover, although the objectives of the manual are meaningful, the current draft of the manual has some flaws and inconsistencies, particularly relating to the institutional framework, and could be revised to clarify the roles and expectations for implementation partners. It may also aim to provide guidance on the reporting cycle and format.

The sub-commission could also increase its role in knowledge management by providing a platform for sharing information between stakeholders involved in rolling out the plan. In addition, formalised partnerships with selected civil society organisations and business representatives may improve oversight of how the Strategy is being carried out.

One way to guide stakeholders and partners is to develop an implementation roadmap, with specific indicators and objectives. Ideally, these indicators and objectives are formulated for each component of the strategy, so the implementation of the strategy can be monitored and evaluated by component. This will help to identify the areas where implementation is on track and the areas that need improvement.

To counter the public perception of corruption, Thailand could strengthen the measurement framework for anti-corruption policies by using policy indicators

At present, the Corruption Perception Index (CPI) is used as a single target indicator in the National Anti-Corruption Strategy, despite its limitations in terms of methodology and usefulness. The CPI score is a composite index combining at least three data sources per country. The confidence intervals are relatively large, and as a result, it is not possible to make scientifically reliable comparisons between countries with similar scores. Such large confidence intervals and the variability of measurements in other countries cast doubt on the reliability of the rankings: if a country falls a few places in the ranking, it may not in fact reflect a real deterioration in the conditions on the ground. Moreover, the CPI score is a national score, and does not reflect regional or sectoral trends and developments. The CPI is thus not suitable as a diagnostic tool. It is a perception index, and it is unclear whether fluctuating perception scores reflect real changes in levels of corruption, or simply general discontent or a response to media exposure of scandals. The CPI is not an appropriate tool for evaluating anti-corruption and integrity policies.

A balanced set of policy indicators could instead be considered, as a framework to replace the CPI as a policy target and as a measure of the progress of the anti-corruption policy. This new set of measurements could assess policy effectiveness, identify areas or institutions at risk, and inform policy planning. Specific indicators can be used to measure budget transparency, integrity in public procurement, efficiency of administrative processes, open government, as well as benchmarks related to organisational integrity, asset declaration systems and whistleblower protection. Moreover, sector-specific indicators can be used to measure integrity in service delivery in health, education or in areas such as licencing or business creation. It may be assumed that these indicators will help improve the CPI score in the long run.

To develop these indicators, Thailand could build on the Integrity and Transparency Assessment (ITA), which can serve as a monitoring and evaluation framework for Thailand's public integrity policies. A monitoring and evaluation system can act as an assurance that integrity policies follow an evidence-based strategic approach, enabling continuous learning (Box 2.1). Evidence from monitoring or evaluation can enhance targeting and steering of current and future policies. This would allow for the detection of challenges and problems in a policy's implementation process (OECD, 2017[2]). Effective monitoring and evaluation create a feedback mechanism between policy design and implementation. On the one hand, they help focus on mainstreaming the public integrity system's strategic goals as the strategy is put in place; on the other hand, this feeds back information from the implementation level to the policy-design stage and enables effective steering, informed decision-making and improved policy design (OECD, 2017[2]).

Monitoring and evaluation strengthen accountability of the public integrity system by making efforts and results measureable. The efforts can be determined as successful or otherwise and can create pressure for change, in benchmarking the different public entities. Making the results available to the public would create additional leverage to promote integrity policies (OECD, 2017[2]).

Box 2.1. Differences in monitoring and evaluation

- **Monitoring** refers to the process of collecting and analysing information on a policy's direct and intermediary ***outputs***. Outputs are the direct results in the sphere immediately affected by the policy. What functions is the policy expected to implement? This question is typically answered on the output level. In some cases, outputs of a policy are self-evident, to the degree that monitoring them becomes redundant. More information might then be obtained by monitoring the ***intermediate output***. Intermediate outputs result from the policy at the first step of corollary influence. This means that they do not automatically result from the policy, but are likely to occur if the policy is implemented as intended. Often, the usage or uptake of an output is a valuable intermediate output to observe.
- **Evaluation**, in turn, explores a policy's mid- and longer-term ***outcomes***. Outcomes are the indirect results of a policy in the final sphere of desired impact. They are indirect, since these outcomes are affected not only by the policy, but also by a range of other variables beyond the control of the implementation process. They tend to capture the effect of a policy on social, economic or organisational variables. Thanks to the multiple factors influencing the desired outcome variable, the causal link between the specific policy and the observed outcome is usually not straightforward (and is referred to as the "attribution gap"). While monitoring is often a continuous function, evaluation involves an effort at measurement specifically set up to investigate a given policy's effect, with a causal attribution.

Source: (OECD, 2017[3]); (Mathisen et al., 2011[4]).

Each integrity policy typically has one or several goals. A goal reflects the change that the policy is intended to bring about. A policy might, for example, have the goal of promoting merit-based recruitment in a public administration unit. The first step of any measurement process is to identify the goals and translate them into objectives. Objectives define the implications of a goal in a specific context. Each objective phrases one aspect of a goal positively and unambiguously in one sentence. Ideally, they provide the who, where, what and when of a goal.

Goals, objectives and indicators can be defined at the level of output as well as outcome. They can also be designed to assess certain qualities of an output or outcome, e.g. the value in relation to an input (Box 2.2) (OECD, 2017[2]).

Box 2.2. Examples of outputs, intermediate outputs and outcome for an Integrity Code policy

Principle 4 of the 2017 OECD Recommendation of Public Integrity calls for "high standards of conduct for public officials" to be set, i.e. through "including integrity standards in the legal system and organisational policies (such as codes of conduct or codes of ethics) to clarify expectations and serve as a basis for disciplinary, administrative, civil and/or criminal investigation and sanctions, as appropriate". One possible measure for achieving this principle is the introduction of an Integrity Code for public officials. This table presents some potential goals, objectives and indicators that an Integrity Code might have on output and outcome level:

	Output	Intermediate Output	Outcome
Goals	Existence of useful Integrity Code	Establish Integrity Code	Establish integrity as an organisational value
Objectives	Integrity Code: • exists • covers all relevant topics • is feasible.	Public officials: • know the Integrity Code and have been trained in using it • initiate discussions on grey areas and ethical dilemmas • suggest solutions. • Managers use the Code as a management tool, e.g. in interviews of candidates for positions in their team, or performance evaluation interviews	Public administration staff model their behaviour and make decisions based on the rules and principles of the Integrity Code.
Example indicator	• Identified risk areas are covered by the code • Staff of all managerial levels have participated in focus groups for development of Integrity Code • ...	• Number of integrity-related suggested improvements • Share of staff working in risk areas who have received risk-specific integrity training • All applicants to a vacant position are provided the Integrity Code, so that they can reflect on it before proceeding in the selection process. • ...	• Integrity measured in staff survey • ...

Source: (OECD, 2017[3]).

It is encouraging that NACC has recently conducted research and analysis on the Corruption Perception Index (CPI) and has provided recommendations on improving the measurement system to the Cabinet. Moreover, PACC is assigned to be the Secretariat of the CPI Improving Committee led by the Deputy Prime Minister, in line with the Office of the Prime Minister Order 112/2559 dated 26 May 2016; PACC reports to the National Anti-Corruption Committee Meeting headed by the Prime Minister.

Thailand may raise the strategic impact of the Integrity and Transparency Assessment (ITA) by fine-tuning its methodology and by linking it with the indicators and objectives of the National Anti-Corruption Strategy

The Integrity and Transparency Assessment is an annual assessment of integrity and transparency at the organisational level across government institutions at the national and provincial levels in Thailand. The assessment methodology has been adapted from the Anti-Corruption and Civil Rights Commission of South Korea, and was then developed and integrated to match with the transparency indicator of NACC. Its implementation in each government department, at the provincial level and in public organisations is led by PACC, partly in partnership with researchers from the Police Academy. Moreover, the implementation in a number of organisations is led by NACC. The ITA is a key element of component Strategy 4, "Development of proactive corruption prevention systems system to counter corruption" of the National Anti-Corruption Strategy, Phase 3 (2017-2021). The third assessment cycle was completed in September 2017.

The methodology consists of three components, combining an internal survey, an external survey for customers/stakeholders, and an evidence-based self-assessment survey, which covers five topics: transparency, accountability, anti-corruption, integrity culture and work integrity. The scores of the ITA surveys are combined in an index, which is published online (Figure 2.2).

Figure 2.2. Integrity and Transparency Assessment – 2015 and 2016 scores from assessment tools

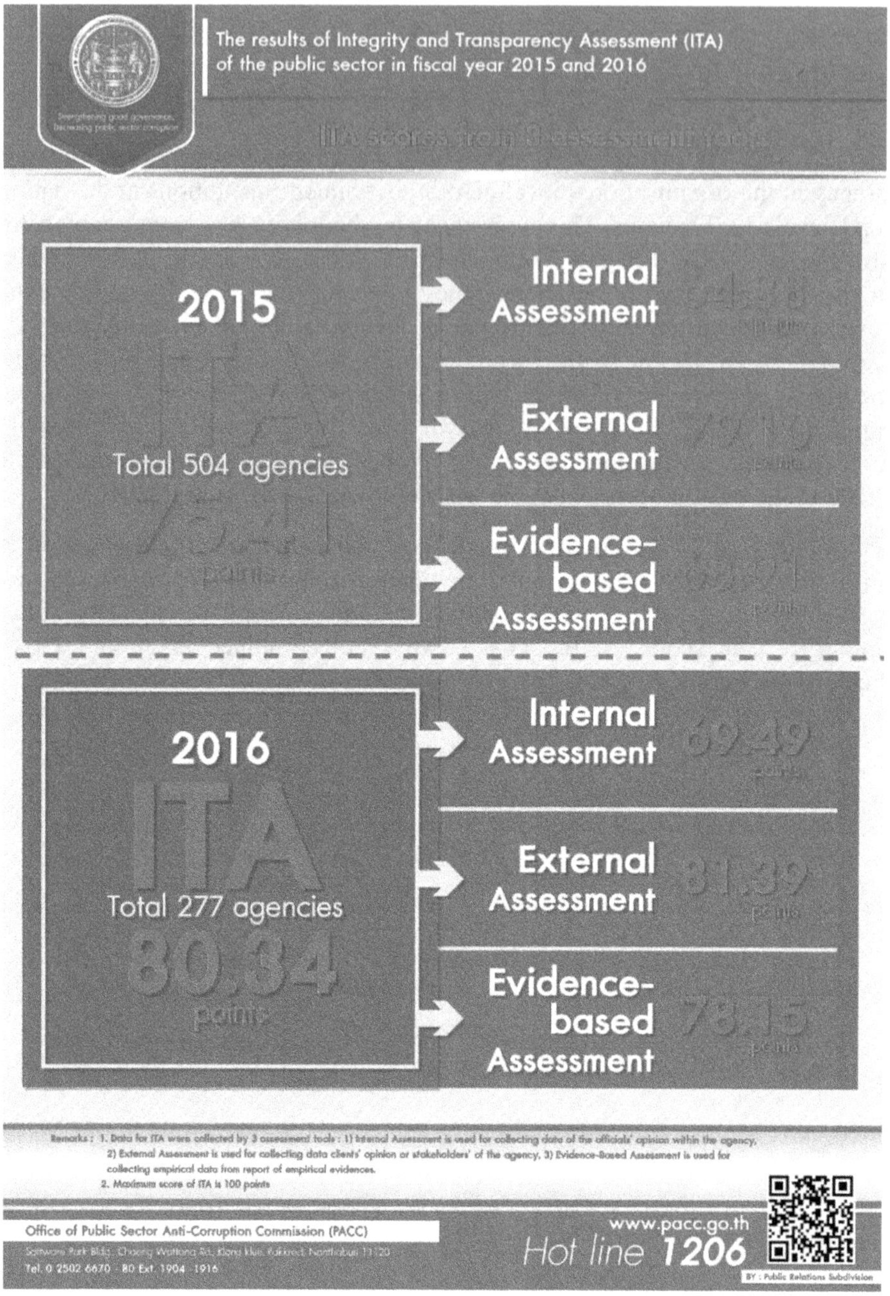

Source: Thailand Today, www.thailandtoday.in.th/node/1084; www.pacc.go.th.

NACC and PACC may need to improve co-ordination on the ITA methodology and implementation. NACC is developing more effective ITA questionnaires and surveys, which follow the government Anti-Corruption policies. In addition, PACC is establishing an action plan for government agencies at the national level, which does not yet cover the provincial level and public organisations; the government plan is to reach a score of 80 for all government agencies by the year 2021. PACC is conducting the assessment training delivery within its own budget. Two working groups have been set up to ensure a more effective implementation and evaluation on the ITA: the Integrity and Transparency Assessment Control and Evaluation Committee and the Integrity and Transparency Assessment Technical and Development Committee. These two working groups may serve as technical exchanges to streamline the efforts of NACC and PACC on the ITA.

The methodology allows for ranking government institutions and comparing scores over time, which makes it an important tool for analysing and comparing the integrity and transparency levels of public entities across the government (Figure 2.3). The ITA also helps identify and support entities and institutions that underperform. For institutions that receive low scores, specific training is offered to their staff. In addition, ITA encourages competitive dynamics among government agencies to promote high integrity standards, and identifies "champions of integrity" in the public sector. These measures are intended to encourage higher standards of integrity throughout government.

Figure 2.3. Integrity and Transparency Assessment – Ranking 2015, 2016

The results of Integrity and Transparency Assessment (ITA) of the public sector in fiscal year 2015 and 2016

TOP 10

2015 (147 agencies)		Rank	2016 (148 agencies)	
Royal Thai Aide-De-Camp Department	89.86 points	1	95.22 points	Royal Thai Aide-De-Camp Department
The Cooperative Promotion Department	84.95 points	2	88.24 points	The Treasury Department
Office of the Higher Education Commission	84.73 points	3	88.22 points	Office of the Permanent Secretary, Ministry of Public Health
Office of the Permanent Secretary, Ministry of Energy	84.62 points	4	87.63 points	The Community Development Department
Office of Justice Affairs	83.78 points	5	87.36 points	Office of His Majesty's Principal Private Secretary
The Treasury Department	83.77 points	6	86.77 points	Office of the Permanent Secretary, Ministry of Defence
Office of the Permanent Secretary, Ministry of Defence	83.69 points	7	86.66 points	Office of the Permanent Secretary, Ministry of Commerce
Office of the Public Sector Development Commission	83.62 points	8	86.55 points	Department of Science Service
Office of His Majesty's Principal Private Secretary	83.38 points	9	86.14 points	Department of Special Investigation
National Statistical Office	83.35 points	10	86.07 points	Office of the Higher Education Commission

Remarks : 1. ITA for department level covered only offices of the agencies located in the central administration and did not cover regional offices of the agencies.
2. Maximum score of ITA is 100 points

Office of Public Sector Anti-Corruption Commission (PACC)

www.pacc.go.th

Hot line 1206

Source: Thailand Today, http://www.thailandtoday.in.th/node/1084; www.pacc.go.th

To further increase its impact, the ITA may fine-tune its methodology and link up with the indicators and objectives of the National Anti-Corruption Strategy. Although the ITA relies on three different sources, the measurement remains largely compliance-oriented, and reportedly, low ITA scores often reflect low motivation or a lack of interest among the staff to complete the self-assessment of the survey, rather than weak integrity systems. It is thus recommended that qualitative integrity elements be integrated into the methodology, such as organisational values, ethical leadership and staff competencies to deal with ethical dilemmas. As in Korea, cases of corruption could also be integrated into the measurement methodology (Box 2.3).

Box 2.3. Annual Integrity Assessment in South Korea

The Korean Anti-Corruption and Civil Rights Commission has successfully employed an innovative initiative for public institutions to assess and disclose their integrity levels on a recurring basis. These periodic assessments aim primarily to:

- recognise corruption-related trends within public organisations;
- identify causes of corruption and corruption-prone areas in public institutions;
- mobilise public organisations to engage in voluntary efforts against corruption;
- provide quantitative data for shaping government-wide anti-corruption strategies.

Assessed areas include individual public organisations and the specific tasks within their scope of activities. The staff of the public organisations and the service users are surveyed on their personal perception of corruption, as well as on their first-hand experience with corrupt practices (e.g. offering money, gifts or favours). The main sources for data collection include telephone or online surveys and statistics on the public servants penalised for corrupt practices. The results obtained from the assessment are presented to relevant public organisations and media.

The 2015 Integrity Assessment included 617 public organisations covering 2 514 lines of work and surveying 245 098 individuals (the majority being public service users). The 2015 Assessment Model was based on the following pillars:

- external integrity: aimed at public service users, it evaluated the degree of transparency and accountability with which their duties were performed;
- internal integrity: aimed at the staff of an organisation, it assessed the level of corruption in institutional practices, managerial activities and organisational culture;
- policy customer evaluation: aimed at policy experts and stakeholders, it evaluated the level of corruption in the processes of establishing and executing policies;
- cases of corruption: calculations of the number of public officials punished or reported in the media for their corrupt acts.

The commission has reported that the scale of the Integrity Assessment activities encourages their impact on the public sector, and that integrity levels in public organisations have continued to improve in the last years.

Source: Presentation by Ms. Sung-sim Min at the meeting of the OECD Working Party of Senior Public Integrity Officials (4 November 2016, Paris).

Interviews with ITA experts show that the ITA information-collectors and report-writers do not always fully understand the objectives and methodology of the ITA. It thus seems necessary to provide guidance and training to those involved in the ITA process, as well as to standardise parts of the data collection process with digital tools, which also helps reduce human errors in data processing.

Thailand could strengthen the impact of the Integrity and Transparency Assessment by providing opportunities for institutional learning and knowledge sharing

Currently, agencies with a low ITA score receive training on integrity policies and the ITA. Support for underperforming entities may include specialised training, and assistance in strengthening internal control units and processes, improving risk management, or setting ethical leadership standards. Although this is encouraging, the impact of the ITA could also be reinforced by creating opportunities for institutional learning based on the ITA. For example, case studies and comparative analysis of entities that perform well could identify good practices, which can be discussed and distributed through the network of Anti-Corruption Operation Centres, publications, online exchange, seminars and training activities. Within the ministries and government agencies, the Anti-Corruption Operation Centres serve as a focal point for the ITA; these are well placed to advise on the specific organisational needs that can strengthen the integrity system.

Furthermore, the ITA has the potential to serve as a monitoring instrument for anti-corruption and integrity policy as a whole. To achieve this aim, it needs to be integrated formally as a policy objective of the National Anti-Corruption Strategy. In the Netherlands, for example, a flexible system of integrity assessments, called the Integrity Monitor, is used to inform and set priorities for the national anti-corruption agenda (Box 2.4).

Box 2.4. Integrity Monitor in the Netherlands' public administration

The Integrity Monitor is an initiative of the Dutch Ministry of the Interior, conducted in close collaboration with the Dutch National Integrity Office and several organisations in the public administration sector (the Local Government Association, the Union of Water Authorities and the Association of Provinces). Since 2004, the Dutch Ministry of the Interior has been regularly monitoring the formal implementation of integrity policies within the public administration. The chief objectives of the Integrity Monitor are:

- to inform Parliament of the status of integrity policies of the Dutch administration and about the actions taken by the Minister of the Interior on the results it reports;
- to engage the decentralised public administrations in taking responsibility for compliance with regulations for integrity policies and for raising ethical awareness;
- to expand the use of the monitoring results to secondary analyses.

Over the years, the Integrity Monitor has evolved substantially. The first Monitor, from 2004, evaluated the implementation of integrity policies among the four levels of public administration. The Ministry's first Monitor took the form of a check-box inventory, and led to the conclusion that public administration entities were not sufficiently implementing the stipulated policies. Clear progress on this front was identified in the 2008 edition of the Integrity Monitor, whose goal was to focus on implementing integrity policies as required by law and related regulations.

As of 2006, perception surveys on integrity policies have been introduced to the Monitor, which laid the foundations for integrative monitoring. An integral approach was introduced in the Integrity Monitor 2012, which consisted of:

- a checklist of integrity policies;
- an inventory of the number of disciplinary cases;
- a perception survey of integrity policies and the integrity culture.

For the first time, the 2012 Monitor also included a perception survey of political office holders.

To reinforce the policies' effectiveness, the 2016 Monitor devoted special attention to integrity, aggression and violence. It targeted groups such as political office holders, secretaries-general, directors and civil servants in central government, the provinces, municipalities and water authorities. Various methods were employed, including *flitspanel* (online panels for government employees), personal e-mails and in-depth research through interviews. The results obtained from the Monitor helped identify priorities for anti-corruption efforts, as well as successful elements of integrity policies, such as commitment at the highest levels of the organisation, leading by example, and shifting from prohibition to awareness within the organisational culture. Enhanced awareness, physical measures (e.g. gates, counters) and the ease of reporting breaches were among the success factors helping to reduce aggression and violence.

Sources: Presentation by Ms. Marja van der Werf at the meeting of the OECD Working Party of Senior Public Integrity Officials (4 November 2016, Paris).
(Lamboo and de Jong, 2016[51]).

Finally, as with the Observatory of Transparency and Anti-Corruption in Colombia (Box 2.5), NACC and PACC may opt to make the ITA data available in Excel format, which makes the information more readily usable for research, comparisons and media reports. Details on the methodology for elaborating the indicators could also be provided.

Box 2.5. The Colombian Observatory of Transparency and Anti-Corruption

The Transparency Secretariat of Colombia has implemented a web portal (the Observatory of Transparency and Anti-Corruption, or *Observatorio de Transparencia y Anticorrupción*) which, among other information management and communication tasks, provides important indicators related to integrity and anti-corruption. The website bundles available information on: *i)* disciplinary, penal and fiscal sanctions; *ii)* the Open Government Index (*Índice de Gobierno Abierto*); and *iii)* the Fiscal Performance Index (*Índice de Desempeño Fiscal*). The data on the penal sanctions comes from the Prosecutor General's Office (*Fiscalía General de la Nación*), the data on disciplinary sanctions from the Attorney General's Office (*Procuradoría General de la Nación*), and the data on fiscal sanctions from the Supreme Audit Institution (*Auditoría General de la República*). The Fiscal Performance Index is elaborated by the National Planning Department (*Departamento Nacional de Planeación*), while the Open Government Index is calculated by the Attorney General's Office.

Additionally, the Observatory's website provides indicators related to Transparency and the implementation status of the Public Anti-Corruption Policy elaborated by the Transparency Secretariat. The indicators related to Transparency include: i) a composite index of accountability; ii) a composite index of the quality of the Corruption Risk Maps; iii) an indicator related to the demand and supply of public information; and iv) a composite index on the Regional Anti-Corruption Commissions (Comisiones Regionales de Moralización). The indicators of the Public Anti-Corruption Policy measure are composite indexes showing the progress made on the policies: i) improving the access to and the quality of public information; ii) increasing the efficiency of the public management tools for preventing corruption; iii) enhancing social control to prevent corruption; iv) promoting a culture of legality in the state and society; and v) reducing impunity in the commission of corrupt practices.

All indicators are also available in Excel format (Open data), which makes the data readily usable for research, comparisons and media reports. Details on the methodology for elaborating the indicators are also provided.

Source: (Colombian Transparency Secretariat,(n.d.)[6]).

To increase the efficiency, coherence and sustainability of anti-corruption initiatives, Thailand could establish a programmatic, multi-year approach to the budget allocation process, for measures and activities underpinning the National Anti-Corruption Strategy

Thailand has a dedicated annual budget to implement the National Anti-Corruption Strategy, which is referred to as the Strategic-Integrated Budget Plan for "Corruption and misconduct prevention and suppression", as one of the 27 strategic-integrated budget plans covering all sectors of society. The budget cycle is based on the fiscal year, and NACC is appointed as main Secretariat host, together with the Bureau of the Budget

(BoB), the Office of the National Economic and Social Development Board (NESDB), the Office of the Public Sector Development Commission (OPDC) and the Office of the National Security Council (ONSC), responsible for developing the budget plans as well as for reporting on the expenditures. The approval process runs from October to October in the next year and involves various steps, which are summarised in Table 2.2.

Table 2.2. Cycle of the strategic-integrated budget plan for fiscal year 2018

	Time frame	Procedures and activities
1	11 October 2016	Cabinet: 1) Approves guideline for budget preparation and timeline for fiscal year 2018 with prioritised strategic-integrated budget plan. 2) Approves report on reviewing linkage within the integrated plan and assign Deputy Prime Minister to chair the Strategic-integrated Budget Preparation Committee, to adopt the review result to be used in budget preparation and to compile targets and indicators from the strategic-integrated plan to report to BoB.
2	21-22 October 2016	BoB, NESDB and OPDC, with the core responsible agency for each strategic-integrated budget plan and relevant agencies, including government agencies and state enterprises, review targets, guidelines and key indicators for fiscal year 2018.
3	21 October 2016	Prime Minister delivers policy in strategic-integrated budget preparation, as well as developing targets, guidelines, and key indicators for fiscal year 2018
4	22 October 2016	Core responsible agency for each strategic-integrated budget plan determines the results from targets, guidelines and key indicators, and reviews and submits them to BoB.
5	25 October 2016	Cabinet: 1) Approves guidelines for strategic-integrated budget preparation, fiscal year 2018; 2) Assesses/appoints the Deputy Prime Minister or the Minister responsible for governing and supervising strategic-integrated budget preparation, fiscal year 2018.
6	27 October- 6 December 2016	Strategic-integrated Budget Preparation Committee meets, fiscal year 2018.
	27-28 October 2016	1) Chairman delivers policy on strategic-integrated budget preparation, assigns responsible agencies, NESDB, OPDC, ONSC, and BoB to set objectives, scope, target, key indicator, guidelines and the relevant agencies.
	27 October-1 November 2016	2) The Committee determines objectives, scope, targets, key indicators, guidelines and relevant agencies.
		3) Government agencies, state enterprises and other agencies prepare strategic-integrated budget proposals and submit them to the Committee.
	14-25 November 2016	4) The Committee determines the strategic-integrated budget proposals, fiscal year 2018, of those agencies.
	28 November- 6 December 2016	5) The Chairman determines and approves the strategic-integrated budget proposals, fiscal year 2018, and submits them to BoB.
7	7 December 2016 – 11 January 2017	BoB determines strategic-integrated budget proposals, fiscal year 2018.
	7-16 December 2016	1) Budgeting Division, BoB, determines strategic-integrated budget proposals, fiscal year 2018, and submits them to the working group.
	19-30 December 2016	2) Working group determines strategic-integrated budget proposals, fiscal year 2018, and submits them to Budget Policy Division, BoB
	4-10 January 2017	3) Budget Policy Division, BoB, conclude and prepare memo on preliminary proposal in Strategic-integrated budget preparation, fiscal year 2018, to report to the Prime Minister.
	11 January 2017	4) BoB reports to the Prime Minister on the overall proposal in Strategic-integrated budget preparation, fiscal year 2018.
8	12 January 2017	BoB informs ministries, government agencies, state enterprises and other agencies to consider this information further for detailed budget preparation, fiscal year 2018.
9	October 2016 – October 2017	Strategic-integrated Budget Preparation Committee, core responsible agency and relevant agencies monitor and evaluate results and inspect budget expenditure.

Note: BoB (Bureau of the Budget); OPDC (Office of the Public Sector Development Commission); NESDB (National Economic and Social Development Board); ONSC (Office of the National Security Council)
Source: Bureau of Budget (October 2016) "Manual for Strategic-Integrated Budget Plan Preparation, Fiscal Year 2018".

To help NACC comply with this process, government institutions involved in anti-corruption and integrity policy are expected to submit their proposals to NACC by August each year. NACC then scrutinises the proposals and prepares a consolidated budget proposal for submission to the Bureau of Budget, the Office of the Public Sector Development Commission and the National Economic and Social Development Board, for further processing and approval.

Although this process sets out a structured framework for budget allocation, it faces a number of challenges:

- The annual approval process is not synchronised with the four-year cycle of the National Anti-Corruption Strategy, Phase 3, 2017-2021. This leaves open the possibility that funded activities may diverge from the activities underwritten by the National Anti-Corruption Strategy, and that some elements of the National Anti-Corruption Strategy receive insufficient funding;
- The annual budget approval makes it difficult for institutional partners to plan multi-year activities, and favours one-off proposals for activities, leaving limited room for sustainability;
- The annual submission of project proposals by various institutional partners results in some incoherence and overlap among the approved activities. It also encourages a degree of competition among partners expected to work together towards the same policy objectives;
- The process requires significant recurrent resources from all institutional partners involved.

To mitigate these problems, Thailand may replace the annual selection and budget allocation process for anti-corruption initiatives with a budget allocated on the basis of the four-year operational work plans that underpin the National Anti-Corruption Strategy. This may increase the coherence of the anti-corruption efforts and further the success of the Strategy, increasing the predictability of the funding, and improving administrative efficiency. An annual review mechanism at the technical level may ensure alignment with the National Anti-Corruption Strategy.

Institutional co-ordination and stakeholder engagement

Thailand may streamline the mandates of NACC, PACC and OCSC and consolidate the mandate for public sector integrity for the executive branch within PACC

In the current Thai institutional context, the mandate and institutional responsibility for corruption prevention in the public sector is spread over several institutions, including NACC, PACC and OCSC. For example, under the Organic Act on Counter Corruption, B.E. 2542, NACC is responsible in areas of corruption prevention for public officials, including values and beliefs for anti-corruption systems and handling conflicts of interest.

Complex co-ordination mechanisms have been established, including technical sub-commissions, but overlap policies and activities remains. There is room for improved efficiency and impact in public ethics, knowledge management, standard setting, awareness raising, capacity building, monitoring and evaluation, asset declarations and corruption reporting.

For example, NACC, PACC, and OCSC undertake integrity-related training activities for civil servants and conduct awareness-raising activities for public officials in a more cost-effective, efficient and coherent manner. These initiatives are parallel to similar activities run by other institutions or have a stand-alone or one-off character, without durable results or impact. Information and good practices are not sufficiently shared, resulting in inconsistent approaches in methods and content. Moreover, no institution is responsible for oversight of all policy measures and activities in corruption prevention in the public sector.

Although NACC is responsible for co-ordinating anti-corruption efforts across all sectors, including the public sector, private sector and civil society, in practice, it is restricted by virtue of its status as an independent quasi-judicial agency. It has only limited leverage in the executive branch to make corruption prevention mainstream and to implement policy measures. Indeed, because institutional partners, and especially high-ranked officials, may be wary of the NACC's investigative mandate, some government institutions are reportedly reluctant to engage with NACC on preventive measures. On the contrary, as part of the executive branch, PACC has a comparative advantage in mobilising public sector actors, and makes a suitable candidate for leading, co-ordinating and mainstreaming the corruption prevention agenda in the executive branch of the public sector. This may yield additional benefits in driving PACC's network of Anti-Corruption Operation Centres, whose main role is to mainstream the question of integrity in line ministries and government institutions. For the judiciary and the legislative branch, NACC may remain the lead agency and co-ordinate its efforts with PACC to ensure policy coherence in the public sector.

Similarly, OCSC conducts activities in corruption prevention, including ethical standard setting in line with the Constitution of Thailand, B.E. 2560, via the Code of Conduct and developing related training materials. OCSC is also responsible for the general training for newly appointed civil servants. As PACC is responsible for educating civil servants on integrity, it would be more efficient to mandate that PACC take on the full package of ethical standard setting and implementation in the executive branch, including via the Code of Conduct, development of related training materials and conducting the training. This transfer may also yield additional benefits in driving PACC's network of Anti-Corruption Operation Centres.

As lead agency for human resources in the public sector, OCSC could focus on integrity in recruitment processes, performance appraisals and career enhancement mechanisms. OCSC, leading the introduction training for new civil servants, may rely on PACC to conduct the ethics module training and provide the training materials.

Thailand may centralise and consolidate the mandate for criminal investigations of corruption cases in the public sector within NACC, to encourage efficiency

As with the corruption prevention mandate, multiple institutions and bodies have a mandate to investigate cases of corruption in the public sector, including NACC, PACC, and the National Administration Centre for Anti-Corruption. NACC is responsible for high-ranking officials, whereas PACC is charged with investigating low-ranked officials (Figure 2.4).

Figure 2.4. Investigative mandates of NACC and PACC

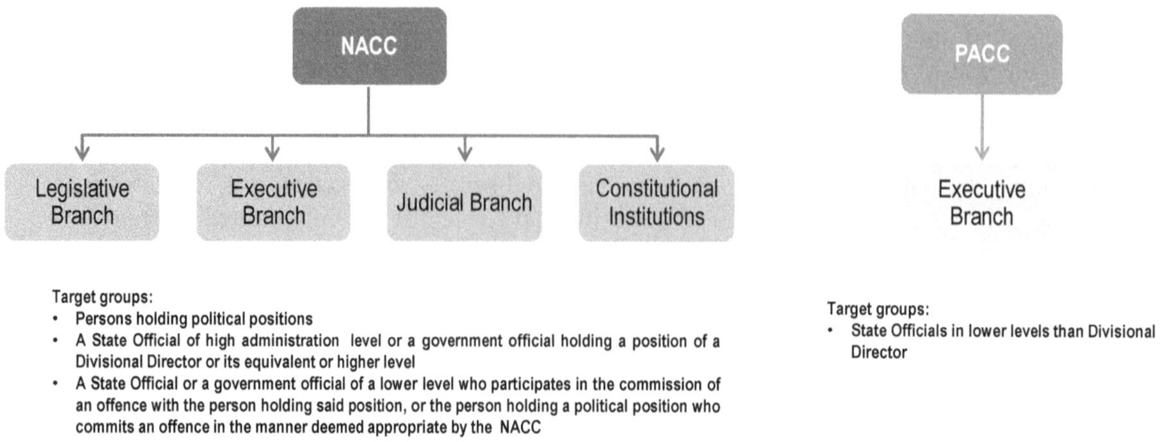

Source: Figure developed from NACC and PACC documentation.

In addition, the National Administration Centre for Anti-Corruption holds certain investigative powers for special cases. Cases are treated by different institutions, depending on the rank or status of the civil servant or public official involved. These agencies have set up similar structures and capacities to conduct investigations, with some duplication of structures and resources. The current institutional setup also results in significant transaction costs in co-ordinating and transferring cases between actors.

Running investigations by one institution may increase efficiency, investigation expertise, management and data security. The investigative mandate is best suited to an institution with a high level of institutional independence, whereas, as explained above, the preventive mandate requires an institution with strong leverage within the executive branch of government. This would make NACC suitable, as the only candidate to hold the investigative mandate for all corruption cases involving public officials. It should be noted that, further down the criminal justice chain, Thailand has several specialised prosecution bodies, including the Criminal Court for Corruption and Misconduct Cases and the Criminal Division for Holders of Political Offices at the Supreme Court of Justice.

Thailand may phase out temporary anti-corruption bodies, such as the National Administration Centre for Anti-Corruption, integrating them into existing structures and mandates

The National Administration Centre for Anti-Corruption was created by Prime Minister Order No. 226/2557 on 24 November 2014 as a temporary anti-corruption body, with PACC as a Secretariat function, reporting to the National Anti-Corruption Committee. The purpose of the Centre is to provide solutions for pressing corruption issues and to deal with corrupt officials in a timely manner. To fulfil these objectives, the Centre has responsibility for corruption prevention and suppression, special investigations, standard setting for anti-corruption prevention and suppression, and developing policy recommendations.

Whereas responsiveness of government structures can be welcomed in general, the creation of the National Administration Centre for Anti-Corruption has added complexity to the already crowded institutional framework and led to duplication of existing institutional roles, both related to corruption prevention and enforcement. This may hamper the operation of existing permanent anti-corruption bodies. Temporary anti-corruption bodies with strong political support carry the risk of political interference, which may jeopardise the objectivity of their operations.

Phasing out the National Administration Centre for Anti-Corruption and integrating its mandate into PACC for the prevention role and into NACC for the investigation and enforcement elements would increase coherence.

To mainstream anti-corruption policies in government institutions, Thailand could increase the capacity of the Anti-Corruption Operation Centres (ACOCs) and co-ordination by PACC

Addressing corruption and promoting public integrity is a responsibility for all government and non-government actors alike. This is articulated in the 2017 OECD Recommendation of the Council on Public Integrity, which calls for a whole-of-government and whole-of-society approach to public integrity. In practice, however, mainstreaming of an anti-corruption agenda across government institutions remains a challenge for many countries across the globe.

In Thailand, ACOCs have been established in line ministries and government institutions. Since their inception in 2012, 35 ACOCs have been installed and are currently operational. ACOCs are to be rolled out across all public institutions and state enterprises at national and provincial levels. Typically, the ACOCs are staffed with two to three employees of the host organisation. A multi-stakeholder committee (led by the Secretary General of PACC) is made up of members from OCSC, NACC, PACC and ACOCs, and serves as co-ordinating body for the ACOCs. The use of ACOCs is a relatively young initiative and their role is still emerging.

The ACOCs provide a good platform for introducing the anti-corruption prevention and ethics policy throughout government institutions. More specifically, they have the potential to provide ethical guidance, awareness-raising, capacity development, monitoring and evaluation, and risk mapping in the public sector. To maximise their impact, the ACOCs may be reinforced in two respects: i) their operational capacity and ii) their strategic role.

As for operational capacity, the ACOC network can be developed as a learning community of public sector integrity advocates. To this end, ACOCs would benefit from support from PACC, in co-operation with OPDC and OCSC, in terms of community building activities, development of technical instruments (such as manuals and training materials) and capacity building (including training the trainers), and exchange of data, knowledge and expertise. PACC is currently in the process of developing a manual with guidelines and procedures for ACOC staff, as well as specific training modules for staff of the respective ACOCs. These efforts could be intensified and supported by an online platform for knowledge management. The example of Austria shows how a network of integrity officials across government institutions can be strengthened through exchange and training in various technical areas (Box 2.6).

Box 2.6. Austrian approach to promoting integrity in the public sector

To mainstream integrity in the public sector, Austria has established the Network of Integrity Officers, which aims to place integrity officers in various federal institutions (e.g. ministries). Tasks performed by the officers include:

- performing advisory services for employees and senior officials;
- circulating information on integrity and awareness raising;
- providing training;
- analysing the risk of corruption;
- collaboration and experience sharing;
- serving as the focal point for compliance-related issues.

The Federal Bureau of Anti-Corruption is responsible for managing the network, generating and collecting scientific expertise and international findings on the topic of integrity, as well as for providing basic training and training materials to the officers. Integrity Officers undergo a comprehensive training composed of 32 teaching units and covering topics such as corruption prevention (national and international prevention instruments), compliance, law and the phenomenon of corruption (background, measurement, risk factors, national and international aspects).

The objectives of developing a sound Network of Integrity Officers include:

- promoting integrity and preventing corruption across sectors;
- restoring public trust in public institutions;
- institutionalising national integrity management;
- sharing experience;
- creating synergy between public entities;
- introducing consistency among national anti-corruption efforts and training.

Since the Network was set up, several advantages of its operation have been identified:

- A public website and an internal communication platform have been developed and maintained by the Bureau.
- Know-how has been smoothly communicated.
- All sectors contribute resources, allowing for their collaborative use.

Source: Presentation by Ms. Martina Koger at the meeting of the OECD Working Party of Senior Public Integrity Officials (4 November 2016, Paris).

In terms of strategic role and mandate, the combination of a preventive and investigative anti-corruption role can be problematic. The investigative mandate may make public officials mistrustful; and their trust and co-operation are essential for mainstreaming the anti-corruption prevention agenda throughout the government. On the investigative side, every government agency contains an Ethics Protection Unit, a body reporting directly to the head of a government agency. This investigates facts concerning ethical violations and reports to the head of a government agency for consideration. In developing the Anti-Corruption Operation Centres, it would thus be preferable to maintain the focus on prevention. In line with this approach, the mandate for corruption reporting, investigations and enforcement needs to be reserved for other specialised bodies, such as the internal audit unit and the Ethics Protection Unit. In Germany, the Contact Persons for

Corruption Prevention can fulfil their advisory role in a spirit of trust; this can in part be attributed to the fact that the Contact Person does not have a role in the complaint-handling process (Box 2.7).

Box 2.7. Germany's Contact Persons for Corruption Prevention

Germany, at the federal level, has institutionalised units for corruption prevention and designated a person responsible for promoting corruption prevention measures within a public entity. The contact person and a deputy must be formally nominated. The Federal Government Directive concerning the Prevention of Corruption in the Federal Administration defines these contact persons and their tasks as follows:

1. A contact person for corruption prevention shall be appointed based on the tasks and size of the agency. One contact person may be responsible for more than one agency. Contact persons may be charged with the following tasks:
   - serving as a contact person for agency staff and management, if necessary without having to go through official channels, along with private persons;
   - advising agency management;
   - keeping staff members informed (e.g. by means of regularly scheduled seminars and presentations);
   - assisting with training;
   - monitoring and assessing any indications of corruption;
   - helping keep the public informed about penalties under public service law and criminal law (preventive effect) while respecting the privacy rights of those concerned.
2. If the contact person becomes aware of facts leading to the reasonable suspicion that a corruption offence has been committed, he or she shall inform the agency management and make recommendations on conducting an internal investigation, on taking measures to prevent concealment and on informing the law enforcement authorities. The agency management shall take the necessary steps to deal with the matter.
3. Contact persons shall not be granted the authority to carry out disciplinary measures; they are not authorised to lead investigations in disciplinary proceedings for corruption cases.
4. Agencies shall provide contact persons promptly and comprehensively with the information needed to perform their duties, particularly with regard to incidents of suspected corruption.
5. In carrying out their duties of corruption prevention, contact persons shall be independent of instructions. They shall have the right to report directly to the head of the agency and may not be subject to discrimination as a result of performing their duties.
6. Even after completing their term of office, contact persons shall not disclose any information they have gained about staff members' personal circumstances; they may, however, provide such information to agency management or personnel management if they have a reasonable suspicion that a corruption offence has been committed. Personal data shall be treated in accordance with the principles of personnel records management.

Source: (Federal Ministry of the Interior, 2014[71]).

To ensure continuity and independence, Thailand may strengthen the merit-based system for appointing NACC commissioners

Anti-corruption is not simply a matter of diagnosing problems and applying solutions. Often, powerful interests will be directly affected by anti-corruption policies and will try to influence decision-making and implementation processes to reduce their reach. Anti-corruption agencies thus need to be shielded from undue political interference. Beyond the risk of undue influence, another reason for shielding anti-corruption agencies from short-term political fluctuations is continuity. Anti-corruption policies, especially preventive measures, usually need time to unfold and show any impact. Even without necessarily following the motive of purposely sabotaging anti-corruption efforts, each change at the head of an agency entails the risk of a change in policies, thus undermining the continuity and coherence of anti-corruption policies. The appointment procedure for the leadership of the NACC is enshrined in the Constitution of the Kingdom of Thailand, B.E. 2560 (2017) (Box 2.8).

Box 2.8. Appointment procedure of the NACC leadership

Constitution of the Kingdom of Thailand, B.E. 2560 (2017), Section 232

- The National Anti-Corruption Commission consists of nine commissioners appointed by the King upon the advice of the Senate from persons selected by the Selection Committee.
- The selected persons must be persons of evident integrity who have knowledge, expertise and experience in the field of law, accounting, economy, administration of State affairs or in any other field beneficial to the prevention and suppression of corruption, and shall have any of the following qualifications:
    - serving or having served in the official service in a position not lower than Chief Justice, Chief Justice of the Administrative Court of First Instance, Chief Justice of the Central Military Court or Director-General of a State Attorney Department for a period of not less than five years;
    - serving or having served in the official service in a position not lower than a Director-General or an equivalent head of the government agency for a period of no less than five years;
    - being or having been in a position of the chief executive of a State enterprise or other State agency which is not a government agency or a State enterprise for a period of no less than five years;
    - holding or having held a position of professor in a university in Thailand for a period of no less than five years, and currently having recognised academic work;
    - being or having been a practitioner of a profession certified by law who has regularly and continuously practiced the profession for a period of no less than 20 years up to the date of nomination, and having been certified by the professional organisation of such a profession;
    - being a person with knowledge, expertise and experience in the field of management, public finance, accounting or enterprise management at the level of no lower than a chief executive of a public company limited for a period of no less than ten years;

- o having been in one of the aforementioned positions for a total period of no less than ten years.

Constitution of the Kingdom of Thailand, B.E. 2560 (2017), Section 233

- The National Anti-Corruption Commissioners shall hold office for a term of seven years as from the date of appointment by the King, and shall serve for only one term.
- During the period in which the National Anti-Corruption Commissioner vacates office prior to the expiration of term and a National Anti-Corruption Commissioner has not yet been appointed to fill the vacancy, the remaining Commissioners may continue to perform duties, unless the number of the remaining Commissioners is fewer than five persons.

Note: Resolution 40/2551 of 15 July, B.E. 2551 (2008), changed the official names of National Counter Corruption Commission and Office of the National Counter Corruption Commission to the National Anti-Corruption Commission (NACC) and Office of the National Anti-Corruption Commission (ONAC) respectively.
Source: Constitution of the Kingdom of Thailand, B.E. 2560 (2017).

The selection procedure for NACC, in accordance with Constitution of the Kingdom of Thailand, B.E. 2560 (2017), and B.E. 2550 (2007), and the rules prescribed in the Organic Act on Counter Corruption, B.E. 2542 (1999), and its amendments stipulate that the Selection Committee shall have the duty to search and prepare a list of 18 selected persons to be nominated to the President of the Senate. Then the President of the Senate shall convoke a sitting of the Senate to pass a resolution to elect the nominated persons, and the voting shall be conducted by secret ballot. The person who receives the highest votes shall be elected as member. In any case, a person nominated to become a member shall be a person who of apparent integrity who does not have a disqualification prescribed by the Organic Act.

Although the procedure stipulates the endorsement of the NACC leadership by the selection committee and by the Senate, whilst mentioning the selection criteria of integrity and other qualifications, interviews with interlocutors from several agencies indicate that the perception exists that the government may weigh in on the appointment of candidates. In OECD countries like Latvia (Box 2.9), an open competition is carried out for the leadership of the anti-corruption agency. The selection commission consists of representatives of state institutions and NGOs, which contributes to the fairness and credibility of the appointment. Similarly, to strengthen its merit-based systems, the Government of Thailand may consider an open competition, involving non-government actors in the selection procedure.

Box 2.9. Latvia's appointment procedure for the head of the anti-corruption agency

In Latvia, pursuant to the Law on Corruption Prevention and Combating Bureau, the Director of the Corruption Prevention and Combating Bureau (KNAB) is appointed by the Saeima (Parliament) on the recommendation of the Cabinet of Ministers, for five years. The Cabinet of Ministers can announce an open competition for this position. Other Bureau officials in managerial positions, such as Deputies of the Director and heads of Divisions, as well as other officials of the KNAB, are appointed and dismissed by the Director. For example, in the process of appointment of the Director in 2004, the Cabinet of Ministers announced an open competition to which 20 candidates applied. The commission selecting candidates was headed by the Prime Minister and consisted of representatives of state institutions and one NGO.

Source: European Partners against Corruption Anti-Corruption Working Group (2008), "Common standards and best practices for anti-corruption agencies", report by the Special Investigation Service (Lithuania) and the Corruption Prevention and Combating Bureau (Latvia).

Thailand could improve co-ordination and effectiveness of anti-corruption policy research by creating a policy research platform

Anti-corruption research brings evidence and insights to make informed decisions for anti-corruption policies, and may also shed light on emerging risk areas, as well as successful approaches to corruption prevention. In Thailand, anti-corruption research is integrated in the National Anti-Corruption Strategy, Phase 3, and currently various agencies and committees contribute to anti-corruption research, including: the Anti-Corruption Research Centre Puey Ungpakorn, NACC's Sanya Dharmasakti Anti-Corruption Institute, PACC, OCSC, the Thailand Development Research Institute, and the Royal Police Cadet Academy.

However, various research initiatives have been undertaken independently, and no overview of existing projects and data or comprehensive research agenda have been put together. A co-ordinated approach may help identify emerging risk areas and link the research agenda with the National Anti-Corruption Strategy and anti-corruption policy objectives.

To ensure more effective policy research, Thailand may consider creating a research platform for co-ordination and the exchange of evidence amongst partnering public sector and academic actors. The platform may feature a website with publications, data sets, calls for projects and information on grant opportunities. The NACC, as the lead agency for anti-corruption across sectors, together with the Anti-Corruption Research Centre Puey Ungpakorn, could serve as a secretariat for this platform, to make sure linkages are established between research and the anti-corruption policy agenda.

To strengthen government accountability and anti-corruption policies, Thailand could reinforce the role of civil society organisations (CSO) in the anti-corruption policy cycle, and support CSO awareness-raising initiatives

Accountability is a cornerstone of good governance. Public officials and institutions must be subject to oversight and accountable for the decisions, effectiveness and performance of policies, as well as the efficient and fair use of public funds. Accountability actors can include autonomous oversight institutions (i.e. electoral bodies, supreme audit institutions, ombudsmen, etc.), as well as the media and civil society. Civil society organisations are particularly important for holding government personnel accountable for their actions and ensuring that government decisions are legitimate, as they represent the diverse interests of the public (The World Bank,(n.d.)[8]).

Civil society plays a key role in influencing and monitoring government, particularly in its efforts in fighting corruption. Specifically, three interrelated mechanisms or roles lead the interplay between the public sector and citizens in promoting a culture of integrity (Figure 2.5):

- Participation in the policy cycle: Citizens can contribute at every stage of the anti-corruption policy cycle, for example via CSO consultation in the development of anti-corruption policies, as is the case in Thailand, or by measuring progress through citizen feedback indicators and mechanisms. In addition, citizens can contribute to good governance in policy implementation and public sector service delivery in various sectors, through reporting channels such as ombudsman services.
- Oversight and accountability: This is the classic "watchdog" role of citizens, where public involvement strengthens the demand for integrity in the public sector and in society as a whole and is supported by CSOs, the media and relevant public institutions, such as supreme audit institutions.
- Awareness-raising: This includes citizen education initiatives, communication campaigns and information exchange with the goal of improving mutual understanding and bringing about change in attitudes and behaviour in the areas of integrity and anti-corruption.

Figure 2.5. Interplay between citizens and the public sector

Citizens

Participation in policy cycle

Oversight and accountability

Awareness raising

Public institutions

Source: (OECD, 2016[9])

To enhance the contribution of CSOs to public integrity, several conditions need to be met. First, when governments call upon citizens and civil society to contribute to policy development, appropriate channels need to be available, effective and reliable. The willingness of the state to engage constructively with CSOs is crucial. Strengthening the relationship between the state and citizens in the fight against corruption will improve the quality of policies by integrating different points of view and enhancing public trust in the government and its actions. A healthy relationship between the government and CSOs can also help the government respond better to changing public trends. CSOs require sufficient resources and flexibility to participate effectively. Second, for citizens and civil society organisations to fulfil an oversight role as a so-called watchdog, data availability needs to be combined with data quality, processing capacity, effective whistleblower protection, and freedom of the press. Third, for civic education initiatives, government institutions and CSOs must tailor awareness-raising initiatives that promote integrity, both in the public sector and in society at large, to specific target groups in order to yield results.

Various civil society organisations in Thailand are working on relevant integrity issues, such as citizen empowerment, natural resources management and private sector integrity. The Anti-Corruption Organisation of Thailand (ACT), originally founded in 2011 as the Anti-Corruption Network, currently comprises over 50 member organisations from various sectors, all of which are committed to the fight against corruption. As mentioned above, civil society organisations are consulted for the development of the National Anti-Corruption Strategy. However, their role in the implementation of the strategy is less formalised or organised. Therefore, guided by the National Anti-Corruption Strategy, Thailand may strengthen co-operation with CSOs in the anti-corruption policy cycle to increase and improve oversight, awareness-raising, capacity development and civic education. To advance this process, Thailand may consider strengthening the Co-operation Centre for Good Governance and Anti-Corruption Promotion, which was established by PACC in 2016 (PACC order No. 218/2559, dated 25 April 2016). This multi-stakeholder initiative focuses on the oversight and awareness-raising roles of CSOs. As this is a relatively recent initiative, the experience of Colombia and Peru may be helpful in designing a suitable format for government-CSO co-operation on public integrity (Box 2.10).

Box 2.10. Government and non-government stakeholders in National Anti-Corruption

Colombia

The Anti-Corruption Statute established the National Committee for Moralisation (NCM), a high-level mechanism to co-ordinate strategies to prevent and fight corruption. The NCM is a multipartite body composed of the President of the Republic, the Inspector General, the Prosecutor General, the Comptroller General, the Auditor General, the head of the Congress and the President of the Supreme Court, amongst others. The NCM is responsible for information and data exchange between the bodies noted above, aiming to fight corruption; it also sets out mandatory indicators to assess transparency in the public administration. It adopts an annual strategy to promote ethical conduct in public administration, including workshops, seminars and pedagogical events on topics such as ethics and public morality, and on the duties and responsibilities of public officials.

The same Anti-Corruption Statute of 2011 created the National Citizens' Committee for the Fight against Corruption (NCCFFC), a body that represents Colombian citizens to assess and improve policies to promote ethical conduct and curb corruption in both the public and private sectors. This committee is composed of representatives from a wide array of sectors, such as business associations, NGOs dedicated to the fight against corruption, universities, media, social audit representatives, the National Planning Council, trade unions and the Colombian Confederation of Freedom of Religion, Awareness and Worship. The NCCFFC issues a yearly report on anti-corruption policy evaluation; promotes codes of conduct for the private sector (in particular on preventing conflict of interest); closely monitors the measures taken in the Anti-Corruption Statute to improve public management, public procurement, the anti-paperwork policy, the democratisation of public administration, access to public information and citizen services; and promotes the active participation of social media in reporting corruption.

Peru

Peru's High-Level Anti-Corruption Commission (*Comisión Alto-nivel de Anti-corrupción*, or CAN) was established by Law No. 29976 and its regulation in Decree No. 089-2013-PCM, which also outlines CAN's mandate and responsibilities. CAN's main activities are: organising efforts; co-ordinating the actions of multiple agencies; and proposing short, medium and long-term policies directed at preventing and curbing corruption in the country.

Like the NCCFFC in Colombia, CAN is formed by public and private institutions and civil society, and co-ordinates efforts and actions intended to combat corruption. Non-governmental actors include representatives of private business entities, labour unions, universities, media and religious institutions. Frequently bringing together diverse stakeholders is intended to encourage horizontal co-ordination and guarantee the coherence of the anti-corruption policy framework, and help protect CAN from undue influence by special interests.

Source: Peru, Law 29976 of 2013, which creates the High-Level Commission against Corruption.

Proposals for action

The institutional arrangement and effective co-ordination among the actors of the public integrity system is a fundamental aspect of Thailand's efforts to enhance integrity and mitigate the risks of corruption at all levels. The OECD thus recommends that Thailand take the following steps to enhance its public integrity system, based on the development, implementation and monitoring of the National Anti-Corruption Strategy, institutional co-ordination and stakeholder engagement:

Development, implementation and monitoring of the National Anti-Corruption Strategy

- To increase the effectiveness of the National Anti-Corruption Strategy, Thailand could reinforce the secretariat function of the NACC Sub-Commission for Strategy Implementation in two ways, by encouraging a multi-stakeholder approach and by developing a monitoring and evaluation framework for the Strategy.
- To help move beyond the public perception of corruption, Thailand could help make the measurement framework for anti-corruption policies more robust by using policy indicators.
- Thailand could raise the strategic impact of the Integrity and Transparency Assessment (ITA) by fine-tuning its methodology and by integrating the ITA scores as indicators in the National Anti-Corruption Strategy.
- To increase the efficiency, coherence and sustainability of its anti-corruption initiatives, Thailand could establish a programmatic and multi-year approach to the budget allocation process, for measures and activities underpinning the National Anti-Corruption Strategy.

Institutional co-ordination and stakeholder engagement

- To enhance the cost-effectiveness, efficiency and impact of corruption prevention efforts at the national level, Thailand could streamline the mandates of NACC, PACC and OCSC and consolidate the mandate for public sector integrity in the executive branch within PACC.
- Thailand could centralise and consolidate the mandate for criminal investigations of corruption cases in the public sector within NACC, to increase efficiency.
- Thailand could consider phasing out temporary anti-corruption bodies, such as the National Administration Centre for Anti-Corruption, and integrate them into the existing structures and mandates.
- To help introduce anti-corruption policies throughout government institutions in a coherent way, Thailand could strengthen the operational capacity of the Anti-Corruption Operation Centres (ACOCs) and their co-ordination by PACC.
- To ensure continuity and independence of institutional operations, Thailand could strengthen the merit-based system for appointing NACC commissioners.
- Thailand could improve co-ordination and effectiveness of anti-corruption policy research by establishing a policy research platform.
- To increase government accountability and the effectiveness of anti-corruption policies, Thailand could reinforce the role of civil society organisations in the anti-corruption policy cycle, including by supporting CSO awareness-raising initiatives.

References

Colombian Transparency Secretariat((n.d.)), *Observatorio de Transparencia*, http://www.anticorrupcion.gov.co/paginas/Indicadores.aspx (accessed on 13 February 2018). [6]

Federal Ministry of the Interior (2014), *Rules on Integrity*, https://www.bmi.bund.de/SharedDocs/downloads/EN/publikationen/2014/rules-on-integrity.pdf?__blob=publicationFile. [7]

Lamboo, T. and J. de Jong (2016), "Monitoring integrity: The development of an integral integrity monitor for public administration in the Netherlands", *Integrity Management in the Public Sector. The Dutch Approach*, https://slidex.tips/download/integrity-management-in-the-public-sector-the-dutch-approach-edited-by-leo-huber. [5]

Mathisen, H. et al. (2011), "How to monitor and evaluate anti-corruption agencies: Guidelines for agencies, donors, and evaluators" U4 Issue No. 8, https://www.u4.no/publications/how-to-monitor-and-evaluate-anti-corruption-agencies-guidelines-for-agencies-donors-and-evaluators-2/. [4]

OECD (2016), *Open Government in Indonesia*, OECD Public Governance Reviews, OECD Publishing, Paris, http://dx.doi.org/10.1787/9789264265905-en. [9]

OECD (2017), *OECD Integrity Scan of Kazakhstan: Preventing Corruption for a Competitive Economy*, OECD Public Governance Reviews, OECD Publishing, Paris, http://dx.doi.org/10.1787/9789264272880-en. [2]

OECD (2017), "Monitoring and Evaluating Integrity Policies", https://one.oecd.org/#/document/GOV/PGC/INT(2017)4/en?_k=vpoh5x. [3]

The Nation (2016), *Prayut carrying burden of anti-corruption fight*, http://www.nationmultimedia.com/news/opinion/today_editorial/30302113. [1]

The World Bank((n.d.)), "Accountability in Governance", https://siteresources.worldbank.org/PUBLICSECTORANDGOVERNANCE/Resources/AccountabilityGovernance.pdf (accessed on 13 February 2018). [8]

Chapter 3. Strengthening public ethics in Thailand

This chapter reviews the Thai policies and practices related to the promotion of a culture of integrity in the public service. In particular, Thailand could strengthen the guidance offered to civil servants on the Code of Professional Ethics for the Civil Service, by assigning to the Public Sector Anti-Corruption Commission (PACC) a role as leading agency for training, advisory and receiving of the Code. Thailand could also mainstream integrity policies in human resource management and ensure the enforcement of integrity standards. Finally, Thailand could improve the monitoring and evaluation framework for integrity policies.

Introduction: Towards a culture of integrity in the public sector

Embedding a culture of integrity in the public sector requires implementing complementary measures. Setting standards of conduct for public officials and the values for the public sector are among the first steps towards safeguarding integrity in the public sector. For instance, international conventions and instruments, such as the 2017 OECD Recommendation on Public Integrity (OECD, 2017[1]) and the United Nations Convention against Corruption (UNCAC), recognise the use of codes of conduct and ethics as tools for articulating the values of the public sector and the conduct expected of public employees in an easily comprehensible, flexible manner. Such instruments can support the creation of a common understanding within the public service and among citizens, as to the behaviour public employees should observe in their daily work, especially when faced with ethical dilemmas or conflict-of-interest situations. Key elements of cultivating a culture of integrity comprise, but are not restricted to:

- investing in integrity leadership to demonstrate a public sector organisation's commitment to integrity;
- promoting a merit-based, professional, public sector dedicated to public-service values and good governance;
- providing sufficient information, training, guidance and timely advice for public officials to apply public integrity standards, including on conflict-of-interest situations and ethical dilemmas, in the workplace;
- supporting an open organisational culture within the public sector responsive to integrity concerns.

In addition, integrity measures are likely to be most effective when they are effectively integrated, or mainstreamed, into general public management policies and practices, especially human resource management and internal control, and when they are supported by sufficient organisational, financial and personal resources and capacities. In turn, high staff turnover, lack of guidance and weak leadership are impediments to an open organisational culture where advice and counselling can be sought to resolve ethical problems.

Thailand faces certain challenges related to the culture of integrity in the public sector, according to recent research on 117 government agencies (Chokprajakchat and Sumretphol, 2017[2]):

- Ethical leadership: A majority of civil servants identified the problem of a lack of commitment at the executive or senior management level. Almost half of the civil servants noted the problem of executives themselves violating the Code.
- Social patronage is reportedly deeply entrenched in the Thai public administration. Around four-fifths (80%) of civil servants noted the problem of social patronage and clientelism.
- Authoritarian and conservative values in the public service may result in a closed organisational culture with little room to discuss ethical situations or dilemmas.

Misconduct appears to a certain degree to be an integral part of the civil service culture, and civil servants acknowledge and self-report various violations of the Code, such as "misuse of public time"; "violation of the official regulations"; "a lack of devotion to duty/use of public time for personal business"; "use of public properties to seek profits for themselves or others".

Thailand could consolidate its anti-corruption training and awareness-raising efforts for the public sector in PACC, which should be the leading agency for drafting and reviewing the Code of Professional Ethics for Civil Servants

In Thailand, the moral and ethical standards for public servants are embedded in the legal and regulatory framework, which describes the minimum obligatory standards and principles of behaviour for civil servants. The laws and regulations state the fundamental values of public service and provide mechanisms for investigation, disciplinary action and prosecution.

- The Constitution of the Kingdom of Thailand, B.E. 2550 (2007)

The 2007 Constitution, Section 279, states that the ethical standard for persons holding political positions, government officials, and state officials of all categories, shall be in conformity with the established Code of Ethics, with the mechanism and system of enforcement, and shall have punishment procedure for each degree of violation. Any violation to comply with the ethical standard will be considered as the breach of discipline. Section 304 prescribes that the codification of ethics should be completed within one year of the promulgation of the Constitution.

- The Public Administration Act B. 2550 (2007)

The public administration, in accordance with the Public Administration Act, expects public agencies to function on principles of good governance; focusing on accountability, promoting public participation, disclosing information and monitoring and evaluating performance.

- The Civil Service Act, B.E. 2551 (2008)

The Civil Service Act (2008), Chapter 5: Upholding the Ethics of Officials, Section 78, prescribes that a civil servant must uphold the ethics of officials as prescribed by the government agency, instilling honour and dignity in officials in the public service (Box 3.1).

Box 3.1. Ethics provisions in the Civil Service Act (2008)

Chapter 5: Upholding the Ethics of Officials

Section 78. A civil servant must uphold the ethics of officials as prescribed by the government agency, with the objective of achieving good officials who exhibit honour and dignity, in particular with respect to the following matters:

(1) adherence to and relentless insistence on taking the correct action;

(2) honesty and responsibility;

(3) transparent and accountable performance of duties;

(4) performance of duties without any unfair discrimination;

(5) result-based determination.

A government agency shall prescribe rules on ethics of officials in accordance with the work descriptions in such government agency, pursuant to technical principles and professional ethics.

When prescribing rules on ethics of officials under Paragraph 2, a hearing shall be held for officials and the rules shall be published for public notice.

Section 79. Where a civil servant fails to comply with the ethical standards stipulated in the Civil Service Act but which does not constitute a breach of discipline, the supervising official shall issue a warning, and take the matter into consideration with regard to appointments, salary increases or to order such official to undergo training.

Source: (Thailand Law Forum, 2008[3]).

- Code of Professional Ethics for the Civil Service (2009)

The Office of the Civil Service Commission, as the leading agency in human resource management of the civil service, introduced the Code of Professional Ethics for Civil Service, promulgated in 2009. The Code provides ten directives of conduct for civil servants. They are summarised in Box 3.2.

Box 3.2. Ten Directives of the Code of Professional Ethics for the Civil Service

1. A civil servant shall hold high moral principles and uphold righteous and moral conduct.
2. A civil servant must have a good conscience and responsibility for duties, devote him/herself to and perform duties with expedition, transparency and accountability.
3. A civil servant must separate personal affairs from office, and uphold the country's public interest above personal gain.
4. A civil servant shall refrain from seeking personal gain in an untoward manner using his/her office, and shall not commit any act in conflict between personal gain and public interest.
5. A civil servant must honestly abide by and comply with the Constitution and the law.
6. A civil servant shall honestly and fairly perform his/her duties, with political neutrality, and serve the people with a friendly disposition and without unfair discrimination.
7. A civil servant must strictly and expeditiously comply with the law on official information, and must not use information that is obtained in the performance of duty for personal gain, but shall provide complete, accurate, up-to-date information for the people.
8. A civil servant must aim for the success of the mission, strictly maintaining quality and professional standards.
9. A civil servant must support the democratic form of government, with the King as head of state.
10. A civil servant must behave in such a way as to preserve his or her reputation and to preserve the dignity of civil servants.

Source: Code of Professional Ethics for the Civil Service (2009).

A country's ethics infrastructure has at its base a legal framework in which laws, regulations and codes define the basic standards of behaviour for public servants and enforce them through disciplinary systems and prosecution. However, the content of legal provisions and policies remains on paper if it is not adequately communicated and instilled. Mechanisms for socialisation and implementation need to be in place for public servants to learn and adopt ethical norms, standards of conduct and public service values.

In Thailand, the Code of Professional Ethics for Civil Servants is relatively well known among civil servants, and most of the ten Directives in the Code are clear and well understood. However, how to apply the principles in daily situations in the professional environment is not fully understood. For a majority of civil servants, the content of the Code is too abstract. (Chokprajakchat and Sumretphol, 2017[2]).

This lack of coherence and co-ordination has impeded the effective transmission of socialisation and implementation mechanisms on integrity to Thai civil servants. NACC, PACC and OCSC provide various types of guidance to civil servants on public ethics and the provisions of the Code of Professional Ethics for Civil Servants. All three organisations conduct training and awareness-raising activities for civil servants. The content, format and quality of the trainings vary, however, and their impact is not measured. Little to no co-ordination occurs on curriculum development, content, training materials and monitoring. Furthermore, OCSC is responsible for the development and review of the Code of Professional Ethics for Civil Servants. PACC is consulted in this review process, but NACC is not, although NACC holds the mandate to formulate ethical standards for the Constitutional Court, independent institutions, and politicians. In addition, PACC manages a network of Anti-Corruption Operation Centres to promote ethical behaviour in line ministries and public institutions. Meanwhile, the OCSC Ethics Promotion Section undertakes similar activities to promote the standards of the Code. The current activities lack coherence in both content and format, and the resources could be spent in a more efficient fashion.

As stated in Chapter 2, PACC should be granted and should consolidate the mandate for public sector integrity. This approach should be applied to public ethics in general, and to the review process of the Code of Professional Ethics for Civil Servants and to ethics training and awareness-raising for civil servants more specifically.

First, this would increase the coherence of the guidance package on integrity provided to civil servants. Similar messages can be replicated through various channels and formats; curriculums and training materials can be built in line with similar content and examples; the review process of the Code of Professional Ethics for Civil Servants may be informed by emerging risks or cases; resources can be used to create new formats, such as online training courses. In this way, PACC can further build its expertise and capacity in offering training, and could provide specific integrity and anti-corruption training to other institutional partners, such as OCSC. For example, OCSC could invite PACC to conduct the training for new civil servants, as part of their induction into the service.

Second, this would maximise the advisory role of the Anti-Corruption Operation Centres across the various government institutions, given that this network is run by PACC. The ACOCs can provide advisory services to civil servants on ethical dilemmas. This advice can be made consistent with the training materials. ACOCs can spot emerging risks or new dilemmas, which can be used in training and inform organisation-specific training modules. It should be noted, however, that the capacity and technical expertise of the ACOCs is limited. Its capacity should be increased if it is to fully exercise its functions.

Third, this would enable PACC to measure the quality and the impact of the training and awareness-raising campaigns. Participants could provide feedback on the quality of the training modules, which can be used for improvements. The training data can also be compared with the evolution of the ITA score and the implementation level of the provisions of the Code, to give an account of the effectiveness of the training.

Consequently, OCSC may focus on integrating public integrity in HRM processes in the public service, such as recruitment and career enhancement. To this extent, the expertise of the OCSC Ethics Promotion Section should re-focus on HRM processes. Alternatively, the capacity of the OCSC Ethics Promotion Section could be integrated into PACC.

Finally, a multi-stakeholder consultation process has not been employed for revising the Code of Professional Ethics for Civil Servants. A sense of ownership could be encouraged by broader consultation among stakeholders, including OCSC, NACC and representatives of line ministries, the private sector and civil society. Because PACC is proposed as the leading agency for public sector integrity, it would take over the role of revising the Code from OCSC, which is currently responsible for this process.

To increase prevention and management of conflicts of interest, Thailand should include a definition of conflict of interest in its Code of Professional Ethics for the Civil Service

Clarity on what constitutes a conflict of interest not only helps civil servants to recognise potential conflicts of interest before they occur, but facilitates the management of conflict- of-interest situations and helps to judge whether a case may be in violation of the Code, for example when considering reporting wrongdoing. A clear definition also helps to apply the same standard across government institutions and ensures policy coherence.

In Thailand, the Code of Professional Ethics for Civil Service (2009) refers to the conflict between private gain and the public interest. Directive IV of the Code of Professional Ethics for Civil Service (2009) stipulates that “A civil servant shall refrain from seeking personal gain in undue manner from using his/her office, and shall not commit any act in conflict between personal gain and public interest”. This provision remains conceptual and provides limited guidance on which situations are in violation of the Code and which are not.

Thailand could refine the concept of conflict of interest in more detail and integrate the definition in the integrity policy framework. For this purpose, it can draw on the experience from OECD countries such as Poland and Portugal, which have embedded a definition of conflict on interest in the regulatory framework (Box 3.3).

Box 3.3. Definitions of conflict of interest in Portugal and Poland

In its 2003 Guidelines for Managing Conflict of Interest in the Public Service, the OECD proposes the following definition: A "conflict of interest" involves a conflict between the public duty and the private interests of a public official, in which the public official has private-capacity interests that could improperly influence the performance of their official duties and responsibilities.

Portugal has established a brief and explanatory definition of conflict of interest in the law: conflict of interest is an opposition stemming from the discharge of duties where public and personal interests converge, involving financial or patrimonial interests of a direct or indirect nature.

Similarly, central European countries have put recent emphasis on providing public officials with a general legal definition applicable across the public service that addresses actual and perceived conflicts of interest. The 2002 Code of Administration Procedure in Poland covers both forms of conflict: a situation of actual conflict of interest arises when an administrative employee has a family or personal relationship with an applicant. A perceived conflict exists where doubts concerning the objectivity of the employee exist.

Source: (OECD, 2004[4]).

To strengthen the application of the Code of Professional Ethics for Civil Service, Thailand should offer civil servants practical examples of ethical dilemmas and include specific guidelines for resolving them

The legislative framework and the Code of Professional Ethics for Civil Service sets out the principles for prevention of conflicts of interest, but too few practical guidelines and examples are available. Although the provisions of the Code are relatively well-known, the understanding of how to apply the principles in daily situations in the professional environment is limited. For a majority of civil servants, the content of the Code is too abstract. As a result, application of the provisions of the Code in the daily work of civil servants remains a challenge, and civil servants struggle to identify ethical dilemmas in a timely fashion and are often unsure about the appropriate response (Chokprajakchat and Sumretphol, 2017[2]). To encourage the uniform application of the Code's provisions, the Anti-Corruption Operation Centres in a number of line ministries (for example, the Ministry of Treasury, Ministry of Commerce), have issued handbooks on dealing with conflicts of interest. This is a promising development, and PACC can also support civil servants in a number of ways:

- map frequently occurring ethical dilemmas and conflict-of-interest situations, for example, related to gift giving, contact with suppliers and recruitment;
- provide examples and practical guidelines on how to solve ethical dilemmas and conflicts of interest. These practical guidelines may be promoted through the network of Anti-Corruption Operation Centres, to support managers and staff of public institutions to efficiently manage and resolve situations that occur frequently;

- Develop in-class and online training modules based on the practical guidelines. Thailand may wish to consider the experience of the region of Flanders in Belgium (Box 3.4).

Box 3.4. Dilemma training in the Flemish Government (Belgium)

In the dilemma training offered by the Agency for Government Employees, public officials are given practical situations in which they confront an ethical choice and where it is not clear how they might resolve the situation with integrity. The facilitator encourages discussion between the participants about how the situation could be resolved, in order to explore the different choices. The debate over the possible courses of action, rather than the solution, is the most important element here, as it will help participants identify different opposing values.

In most training courses, the facilitator uses a card system. The rules are explained and participants receive four option cards, bearing the numbers 1, 2, 3 or 4. The dilemma cards are then placed on the table. The dilemma cards describe the situation and give four options on how to resolve the dilemma. In each round, a participant reads out the dilemma and options. Participants each indicate their choices with the option cards and explain the motivation behind their choice. Participants then discuss the different choices. The facilitator remains neutral, encourages debate and suggests alternative ways to approach the dilemma (e.g. the sequence of events and boundaries for unacceptable behaviour).

One example of a dilemma situation that could arise would be:

I am a policy officer. The minister needs a briefing within the next hour. I have been working on this matter for the last two weeks and it should already have been finished. However, the information is not complete. I am still waiting for a contribution from another department to verify the data. My boss asks me to submit the briefing urgently, because the chief of cabinet has already called. What should I do?

- I send the briefing and do not mention the missing information.
- I send the briefing, but mention that no decisions should be made based on it.
- I do not send the briefing. If anyone asks about it, I will blame the other department.
- I do not send the information and come up with a pretext and a promise to send on the briefing tomorrow.

Other dilemma situations could cover the themes of conflicts of interest, ethics, loyalty, leadership etc. The training and situations used can be targeted to specific groups or entities.

For example:

You are working in Internal Control and are asked to be a guest lecturer in a training programme organised by the employers of a sector that is within your realm of responsibility. You will be well paid, make some meaningful contacts and learn from the experience.

Source: Website of the Flemish Government, https://overheid.vlaanderen.be/omgaan-met-integriteitsdilemmas (in Dutch).

To strengthen compliance with the provisions of the Code of Professional Ethics for Civil Service, PACC and OCSC could disseminate information on the available and the applied sanctions for misconduct

Sanctions can have a deterrent effect and encourage civil servants to follow the provisions of the Code of Professional Ethics for Civil Service. For this mechanism to work, it is necessary for civil servants to know that sanctions may be applied in case of misconduct, and also that these sanctions are in fact being applied. If not, a culture of apparent impunity may undermine the potential power of sanctions.

In Thailand, the Civil Service Act, B.E. 2551 (2008), Chapter 6 is dedicated to the disciplinary regime, including reasons for disciplinary measures and possible punishment (Box 3.5). Chapter 9 describes the disciplinary proceedings, including the investigation and possibilities for appeal.

Box 3.5. Disciplinary punishment in the Civil Service Act, B.E. 2551 (2008)

Chapter 6: Discipline and Maintenance of Discipline

Section 88. A civil servant who commits a breach of discipline must receive a disciplinary punishment, unless there is reasonable cause for exempting punishment, as provided in Chapter 7, Disciplinary Proceedings. There are five modes of disciplinary punishment, as follows:

(1) written reprimand;

(2) deduction of salary;

(3) reduction of salary;

(4) dismissal;

(5) expulsion.

Source: (Thailand Law Forum, 2008[5]).

These provisions are little-known by civil servants. More than half of civil servants report that there have not been informed or that they do not know whether their agencies have prescribed punitive measures against violators (Chokprajakchat and Sumretphol, 2017[2]). Therefore, PACC could integrate the topic of disciplinary measures and sanctions as part of the awareness-raising efforts and ethics training for civil servants.

According to the Civil Service Act, the OCSC Bureau for Disciplinary Standards is responsible for penalising civil servants. The number of cases per year is classified information, but OCSC reportedly deals with approximately 100 to 300 cases per year. OCSC has published anonymised examples of cases of disciplinary punishment in *The Guidelines for Disciplinary Punishment*. Quite apart from the examples, a number of benefits and reasons can justify publishing generic statistics and characteristics on all cases:

- The data can provide evidence on particular risks related to specific sectors and/or organisations;
- Information about the sanctions and the response of management will help dispel the notion of perceived impunity;

- Information on the management responses will encourage public institutions to go beyond individual measures and to take structural measures to prevent similar cases in the future;
- Public accountability of the OCSC.

Under the leadership of NACC and in consultation with PACC, a systematic review of the implementation of the Code across government agencies should be integrated in the annual Integrity and Transparency Assessment (ITA) of government

The implementation of the Code is currently not linked with the annual ITA or with the National Anti-Corruption Strategy objectives. A decision to link them would offer certain advantages. First, if implementing the Code is integrated into the annual ITA, better results can be expected from the implementation of the Code. Indeed, studies have found that measuring the implementation of the Code helps reduce integrity violations. In agencies that do not assess the implementation of the Code, violations of the Code were higher. Measuring the response can draw the attention of civil servants to the Code and its provisions, and at the same time send a signal that the implementation of the Code is relevant (Chokprajakchat and Sumretphol, 2017[2]). Two mutually reinforcing impulses play a role: the measuring draws the attention of civil servants to the Code and its provisions, and simultaneously sends a signal that the implementation of the Code is relevant.

Second, this would reinforce and balance the ITA, as new data on the actual ethical behaviour of civil servants filled out the picture. This approach would counter the possible criticism that ITA is now merely a check-the-box exercise that reveals little about the rollout of the ethics framework.

Third, because the National Anti-Corruption Strategy lacks indicators related to organisational integrity in the public sector, adding the assessment of the implementation of the Code to the ITA could fill this gap. The data about the implementation of the Code may cover the degree of staff members trained on integrity issues, passing a knowledge test about the code, using the gift policy arrangements. The ITA framework, including data on the implementation of the Code, can serve as indicators for organisational integrity in the public service, and would make it possible to set specific targets. In this way, integrity policy could be monitored and adjusted where needed.

NACC, as leading agency for the design of the ITA and for the National Anti-Corruption Strategy, should lead this effort and explore the feasibility and practical next steps in co-operation with PACC, which is implementing the ITA.

The ITA, including the implementation of the Code, may serve as a key performance indicator of public institutions, aligning the organisational objectives with the integrity policy framework. This would send a strong signal that integrity and organisational performance are mutually reinforcing, and it would help mainstreaming integrity policy in the daily operation of the organisation. As a good practice for mainstreaming integrity policy across government institutions, a number of OECD and partner countries have adopted the practice of tailored corruption prevention plans for ministries and government agencies. The ITA could be the starting point for developing such an approach in Thailand.

Since human resources management (HRM) practices may contribute to public sector integrity, OCSC could consider further mainstreaming integrity in human resources processes in the civil service, including in recruitment and career enhancement

Public ethics and the management of conflicts of interest are about directly or indirectly changing the behaviour of an organisation's human resources. HRM policies are part of both the problem and the solution of promoting integrity in public administration. Factors such as a high level of politicisation that encourages loyalty not to the public but to the party or "patron" in power, a low culture of performance orientation, poor rewards and salaries, low levels of contract security, a lack of training and professionalism, a high staff turnover, lack of guidance and a lack of commitment from the highest levels are impediments to an open organisational culture where advice and counselling can be sought to resolve ethical problems. This can lead to opportunities for and rationalisation of corrupt practices, and also to low levels of integrity. If staff rotation is high, less importance may be attached to a strong ethics culture in the workplace, since employees are not employed for long enough to feel engaged with public integrity values and apply them in practice.

In Thailand, human resources processes are separated from the public integrity agenda, and integrity measures are not yet reflected in HR processes of recruitment and career enhancement. With reference to the Civil Service Act, OCSC has a leading role in human resources management in the public sector and thus has leverage to promote integrity in HRM processes throughout government institutions. Table 3.1 provides an overview of possible measures:

Table 3.1. Mainstreaming integrity throughout HRM processes

HRM practices	Mainstreaming integrity
Human resources planning	Assessing integrity risks of different positions and planning accordingly
Entry into public service	Background checks, ethical tests, managing potential conflicts of interest arising from previous employment (revolving doors); developing job descriptions with ethical considerations in mind
Professional development, training and capabilities certification	Customised training on integrity policies
Performance evaluation and career enhancement	For managers: assessing their management of employees' conflict-of-interest or ethical dilemmas For employees: assessing adherence and compliance with integrity policies
Severance and exit from public service	Monitoring potential conflicts of interest arising from the nature of the next employment (i.e.the "revolving door")

Two key areas deserve particular attention: recruitment and performance evaluations. The recruitment process offers the first point of contact between the employer and potential future employees. Ideally, the employer would like to ensure, in addition to the usual criteria, that the candidates conduct themselves with integrity and understand and agree to the ethical principles and values of the public service. Procedures at this stage typically consist of background checks with past employers and checking criminal and disciplinary records, but there is also a need to state clearly what is expected from the future public servants in terms of values and behaviour. Australia provides a good example of mainstreaming integrity in recruitment (Box 3.6).

Box 3.6. Recruitment processes and integrity: Experience from Australia

"Filters" can be built into a recruitment process to ensure that applicants are tailored to the organisation's requirements. In Australia, for example, one agency analysed disciplinary issues amongst new recruits after 12 months on the job and identified a need to better manage indicators of integrity earlier in the selection process.

As a result, interventions were then instituted at important stages:

- A question-and-answer survey was included as part of the general information for potential applicants. It asked questions about how people felt about certain working conditions and interactions. Based on an indicative score, potential applicants were then encouraged to proceed to the next stage or encouraged to speak about the role with people who knew them well before proceeding to the next stage. This supported self-selection by applicants.
- As part of the online application, more targeted integrity questions were asked about their background and experience, for example, questions about dealing with authority, diverse cultures and financial management. This provided baseline data for comparative purposes.
- Successful applicants in the technical assessment phase were asked to retake the integrity questions. Experts were asked to identify discrepancies or anomalies between the data sets, and individually followed these up with applicants. The delay between administering the questions increased the validity of the data.
- Only applicants who successfully passed both the technical and the integrity phases were invited to face-to-face interviews, which included a practical role play.

The outcome was a considerable reduction in disciplinary issues and increased retention rates for new recruits.

Source: Input provided by the Australian Merit Commissioner, June 2016.

The regular performance evaluations conducted by the responsible public managers and their staff offers an important entry point for integrity policies. Thailand could aim at a stronger involvement of public managers with staff responsibility, providing specific training and clear guidelines on how they should exercise judgement when cases are brought to them, how to signal unethical behaviour in discussions with their staff, how to promote a culture of open discussion, and how to resolve conflicts of interest. Performance evaluations can be used to transmit values and expectations, although they are usually focused only on the past objectives and future goals of employees.

At such meetings it can be helpful to explicitly address the subject of public ethics and conflicts of interest, tailored to the specific job profile and related risk areas (for example recruitment, procurement, accounting etc). In this way, the meeting goes beyond the evaluating past performance. If taken seriously, and not as a check-box exercise, regular discussions of this kind would provide the opportunity to set the tone from the top. Including integrity in the criteria for the professional development of the public servants could also be considered.

To strengthen integrity in the legislative branch, Thailand could increase the effectiveness of integrity policies of the House of Representative and the Senate, including in developing and implementing the code of ethics

Both the House of Representatives and the Senate are independent bodies with their own integrity policy, including a Code of Conduct. However, the Code of Conduct does not stipulate preventive or administrative rules for prohibitions or restrictions for members of parliament (MPs) to accept gifts and other advantages, or a specific procedure to follow for reporting and authorising, for declaring or for returning undesired or unacceptable benefits. Moreover, in the development process of the code of conduct, the implementation as well as for sanctioning, an Ethics Committee solely composed of members of the House of Representatives and the Senate is involved, which may lead to a culture of self-protection and impunity. It is telling that the Ethics Committee has issued not one sanction to date.

It is thus recommended that Thailand reinforce integrity policies of the House of Representative and the Senate, which can be done in various ways. First, the Code of Conduct can be amended to include a gift policy for MPs, for example through restrictions and a gift registry. Second, although the current approach of an Ethics Committee is common throughout the world, Thailand would appoint an integrity officer to deal with the implementation and monitoring of the Code of Conduct in the House of Representatives and the Senate. The integrity officer can help to ensure that integrity standards are maintained across legislatures and composition of the parliament. Examples include the United Kingdom's Parliament and Queensland's Parliament in Australia (Box 3.7).

Box 3.7. Integrity Officers in Parliament

Parliamentary Commissioner for Standards in the United Kingdom

In the United Kingdom, the Office of the Parliamentary Commissioner for Standards deals with the application of the Code of Conduct and related rules that apply to Members of Parliament. The Parliamentary Commissioner for Standards is appointed for a fixed term of five years and is an independent officer of the House. The Commissioner's key responsibilities include:

- overseeing the operation of the Register of Members' Financial Interests;
- advising the Committee on Standards about the interpretation of the Code of Conduct and, if necessary, proposing changes to the Code;
- providing confidential advice, guidance and training for MPs on matters of conduct and ethics;
- producing an annual report to the House of Commons on their findings.

The Commissioner can also investigate allegations that a named member has breached the rules contained in the Code of Conduct. These findings are then reported to the Committee on Standards to adjudicate and to recommend any appropriate sanction.

Queensland Integrity Commissioner

The Queensland Integrity Commissioner is an independent officer of the Queensland Parliament responsible for providing advice on issues of ethics and integrity, and for overseeing the lobbying register.

Under the Integrity Act 2009, the Commissioner can issue written advice to Ministers, MPs, senior civil servants and other government employees about ethics and integrity-related issues. For example, the Commissioner can offer advice and guidance on conflicts of interest or meet with individual MPs to discuss any issues that may arise in relation their declaration of financial interests. As well as maintaining the lobbying register, the Commissioner also monitors compliance by lobbyists and government with the Integrity Act and the Lobbyist Code of Conduct.

Sources: (UK Parliament,(n.d.)[6]); (Queensland Integrity Commissioner,(n.d.)[7]).

Proposals for action

- To provide a coherent and cost-effective guidance package for civil servants on public ethics, Thailand should consolidate its anti-corruption training and awareness raising efforts for the public sector within the Public Sector Anti-Corruption Commission (PACC). Similarly, PACC should be the leading agency for drafting and reviewing the Code of Professional Ethics for Civil Servants.
- To allow effective prevention and management of conflicts of interest, Thailand should integrate a definition of conflict of interest in its Code of Professional Ethics for the Civil Service.
- To strengthen the observance of the Code of Professional Ethics for Civil Service, Thailand should guide civil servants with practical examples of ethical dilemmas, and include specific guidelines for resolving them.
- To increase compliance with the provisions of the Code of Professional Ethics for Civil Service, PACC and the Office of the Civil Service Commission (OCSC) could disseminate information on both the sanctions available and the sanctions applied for misconduct.
- Under the leadership of National Anti-Corruption Commission (NACC) and in consultation with PACC, a systematic review of the implementation of the Code across government agencies should be included in the annual Integrity and Transparency Assessment (ITA) of government institutions and should be linked with the National Anti-Corruption Strategy objectives.
- As HRM practices may help contribute to public sector integrity, OCSC could consider further mainstreaming integrity in human resources processes in the civil service, including in recruitment and career enhancement.
- To encourage accountability, Thailand could strengthen the effectiveness of integrity policies of the House of Representatives and the Senate, by developing and implementing the code of ethics.

References

Chokprajakchat, S. and N. Sumretphol (2017), "Implementation of the code of professional ethics for Thai civil servants", *Kasetsart Journal of Social Sciences*, Vol. 38, pp. 129-135, http://dx.doi.org/10.1016/j.kjss.2016.03.004. [2]

OECD (2004), *Managing Conflict of Interest in the Public Service: OECD Guidelines and Country Experiences*, OECD Publishing, Paris, http://dx.doi.org/10.1787/9789264104938-en. [4]

OECD (2017), *OECD Recommendation of the Council on Public Integrity*, http://www.oecd.org/gov/ethics/Recommendation-Public-Integrity.pdf. [1]

Queensland Integrity Commissioner((n.d.)), *Commissioner profile*, https://www.integrity.qld.gov.au/about-us/commissioner-profile.aspx (accessed on 13 February 2018). [7]

Thailand Law Forum (2008), *Civil Service Act Thailand, chapter 5, sections 78 and 79*, http://www.thailawforum.com/database1/civil-service-act-10.html. [3]

Thailand Law Forum (2008), *Civil Service Act Thailand, B.E. 2551, chapter 6, section 88*, http://www.thailawforum.com/database1/civil-service-act-11.html. [5]

UK Parliament((n.d.)), *Parliamentary Commissioner for Standards Office*, http://www.parliament.uk/mps-lords-and-offices/standards-and-financial-interests/parliamentary-commissioner-for-standards/parliamentary-commissioner-for-standards/ (accessed on 13 February 2018). [6]

Chapter 4. Reinforcing public sector integrity in Thailand by managing conflicts of interest

This chapter examines the Thai integrity system in relation to the management of conflict-of-interest and asset disclosure. In line with the recommendations of the previous chapters, Thailand may consider consolidating the mandate for managing conflicts of interest of all civil servants within the Public Sector Anti-Corruption Commission (PACC) and developing more detailed measures, such as specific guidance for categories of public officials who may be at greatest risk, as well as a monitoring system for the cooling-off period. The scope of asset disclosure could be expanded to include senior public officials and other at-risk officials, while strengthening the auditing capacity of the National Anti-Corruption Commission (NACC) with online technology. Thailand could also consider making asset disclosure forms publicly accessible for public scrutiny gradually and progressively.

The statistical data for Israel are supplied by and under the responsibility of the relevant Israeli authorities. The use of such data by the OECD is without prejudice to the status of the Golan Heights, East Jerusalem and Israeli settlements in the West Bank under the terms of international law.

Management of conflicts of interest and asset declaration

Ensuring that the integrity of government decision-making is not compromised by public officials' private interests has become a growing concern across OECD member countries. A conflict of interest arises when a public official's private interests may improperly influence the performance of official duties. The varying approaches to managing conflict-of-interest situations in different countries often reflect their legal and public service traditions. In most countries, institutional measures such as external audit and verification and other internal supervisory approaches are widely observed, while asset and private interest disclosure by senior public officials continues to be an essential tool for managing conflicts of interest. A modern conflict-of-interest policy should seek to strike a balance. Conflicts of interest, if they are not adequately identified and managed, may lead to corruption. At the same time, an excessively strict approach can be costly and unworkable, and may deter experienced and competent potential candidates from entering the public service. The OECD Guidelines for Managing Conflict of Interest in the Public Service provide policy makers with a set of tangible policy options based on promoting individual responsibility, supporting scrutiny and creating an appropriate organisational culture.

In Thailand, the Organic Act on Counter Corruption, B.E. 2542, currently provides the legal framework for managing conflicts of interest. Sections 100-103 of the Act especially deal with conflicts between personal interest and the public interest (Box 4.1). In addition, the Notification of the National Anti-Corruption Commission on the criteria for accepting assets or other benefits according to the code of conduct of state officials, B.E.2543, Regulation of the Prime Minister's Office, on giving or receiving gifts for state officials, B.E. 2554, and Cabinet Resolution of 4 December 2001, B.E. 2544, also provide complementary provisions for managing conflicts of interest in the public sector.

Box 4.1. The Organic Act on Counter Corruption, B.E. 2542

CHAPTER IX

Conflicts Between Personal Interest and Public Interest

Section 100. Any State Official shall not carry out the following acts:

(1) being a party to or having interest in a contract made with a Government agency where such State Official performs duties in the capacity as State Official who has the power to conduct supervision, control, inspection or legal proceedings;

(2) being a partner or shareholder in a partnership or company which is a party to a contract made with a Government agency where such State Official performs duties in the capacity as a State Official who has the power to conduct supervision, control, inspection or legal proceedings;

(3) being a concessionaire or continuing to hold a concession from the State, State agency, State enterprise or local administration or being a party to a contract of a directly or indirectly monopolistic nature made with the State, a Government agency, State agency, State enterprise or local administration, or being a partner or shareholder in a partnership or company which is a concessionaire or a contractual party in such manner;

(4) being interested in the capacity as a director, counsel, representative, official or employee in a private business which is under supervision, control or audit of the State agency to which such State Official is attached or where such State Official performs duties in the capacity as State Official, provided that the nature of the interest of the private business may be contrary to or inconsistent with public interest or the interest of the Government service or may affect the autonomy in the performance of duties of such State Official.

The positions of State Officials prohibited from carrying out the activities under Paragraph 1 shall be prescribed and published in the Government Gazette by the National Anti-Corruption Commission (NACC).

The provisions of Paragraph 1 shall apply to spouses of the State Officials under Paragraph 2. For this purpose, the activities carried out by the spouse shall be deemed to be the activities carried out by the State Official.

Section 101. The provisions of Section 100 shall apply *mutatis mutandis* to the activities carried out by the person who has already ceased to be a State Official for less than two years, with the exception of the holding of shares of not more than 5 percent of the total number of shares issued by a public limited company which is not a party to a contract made with the State agency under Section 100 (2), for which permission is obtained under the law on securities and securities exchange.

Section 102. The provisions of Section 100 shall not apply to the carrying out of activities of the State Official who is entrusted by the Government agency having the power to supervise, control or inspect the operation of a limited company or a public limited company to perform duties in the limited company or public limited company in which the State agency holds shares, or with which it participates in an undertaking.

Section 103. Any State Official shall not receive property or any other benefit from any person other than the legitimate property or benefit derived under the law, rules or regulations issued by virtue of the provisions of law, with the exception of the acceptance of the property or any other benefit on the ethical basis in accordance with the rules and in such amount as prescribed by the NACC.

The provisions of Paragraph 1 shall apply *mutatis mutandis* to the acceptance of property or any other benefit by the person who has ceased to be a State Official for less than two years.

Source: The Organic Act on Counter Corruption, B.E. 2542, https://www.oecd.org/site/adboecdanti-corruptioninitiative/46817329.pdf.

Thailand could consider consolidating the mandate for public sector integrity, making PACC the agency responsible for conflict-of-interest policies for all civil servants

The organisation can be proactive in helping its employees identify and manage emerging conflicts of interest by enabling participants in official decision-making capacities to foresee potential conflicts where feasible, for example by setting clear definitions and procedures for managing and resolving conflicts of interest. Likewise, providing customised training on the conflict-of-interest provisions and options for management can help employees identify and deal with potential conflict-of-interest situations at an early stage and encourage them to come forward with conflicts of interest. Establishing clear institutional responsibility for ensuring coherence in such policies and guidelines across the government lays a strong foundation for managing conflicts of interest in the public sector.

Under the current setting in Thailand, Sections 100-103 of the Organic Act on Counter Corruption, B.E. 2542, lists the situations that state officials should avoid in order to manage conflict of interest. NACC is responsible for implementing the conflict of interest policies governed under the Act, and also provides a guideline with practical examples to inform the public officials. For example, according to the Law on Procedure for Giving and Taking Any Gifts for Public Officials, B.E. 2544, and the Practical Guidelines for Public Officials, B.E. 2543, public officials are not permitted to receive a gift worth more than THB 3 000 (approximately EUR 78). Such guidelines are also available on a mobile application. NACC also publishes operation guidelines on Section 100 and 103 for state officials. NACC provides a mobile application as an alternative channel, aiming to educate state officials, especially those working in local administration, and the general public on the guidelines for conflict of interest set out in Section 100, Section 103 of the Organic Act on Counter Corruption, B.E. 2542, and the Law Prohibiting State Officials from Receiving Assets or Other Benefits from Outsiders (Box 4.2). In addition, the issue of conflict of interest is addressed in the Guidelines on Monitoring Corrupt Government Officials, Vol. 3, published by NACC.

Box 4.2. NACC's e-learning mobile application on Sections 100 and 103 of the Organic Act on Counter Corruption, B.E. 2542

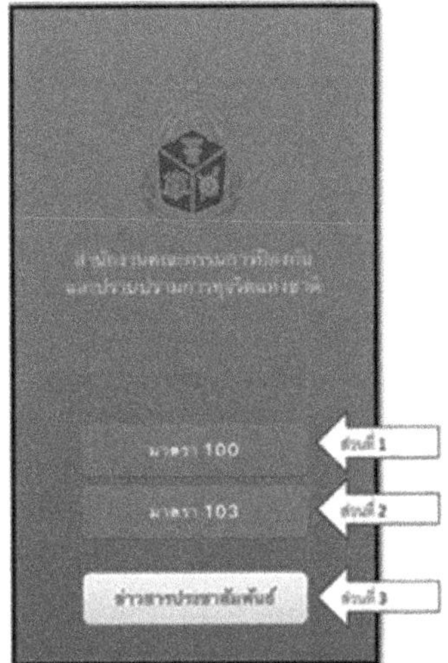

Online self-test

Register with 13-digit personal ID.

The test is divided into three levels:

- Fundamental level
- Intermediate level
- Advanced level

Each level has 15 multiple-choice questions.

Content:

Part 1: Section 100

Part 2: Section 103

Part 3: News

An **E-Certificate** is provided via email when a score of 80% or above is achieved.

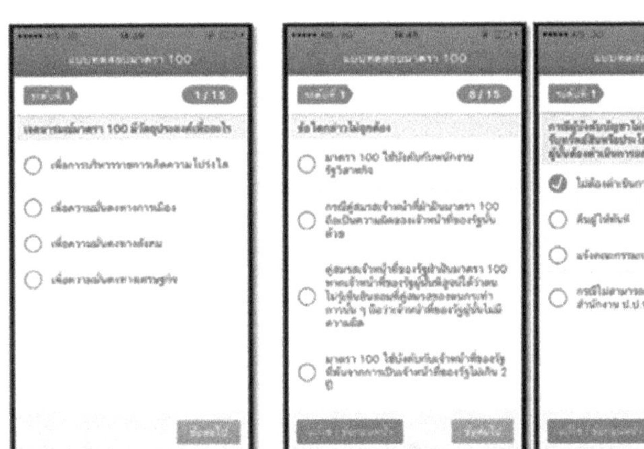

Source: National Anti-Corruption Commission.

While NACC's leadership in providing manuals and online application to ensure proper understanding of conflict of interest is in line with good practices of many OECD countries, analysis and recommendations of previous chapters highlighted the value of streamlining the mandate for public sector integrity within PACC. Managing conflicts of interest is closely linked to the Code of Professional Ethics for Civil Servants. Ethical training for civil servants, and the direct involvement and co-operation of PACC, would thus be more cost-effective and efficient while NACC continues to be responsible for parliamentarians and other officials in the legislative and judicial branches. To this end, PACC, in consultation with NACC, could be the leading agency for maintaining conflict-of-interest policies for all the civil servants in the public sector, to increase the coherence of the guidance package on integrity provided to civil servants.

Thailand could consider developing specific guidance for categories of public officials who are at risk due to the nature of their work

The role of ensuring clear guidance also involves considering the specific risks associated with the administrative functions and sectors most exposed to corruption. As different organisations face different contexts, and as the nature of their work varies, they may also be faced with distinctive ethical dilemmas and specific conflict-of-interest situations. While the ultimate responsibility falls on the individual public official to recognise in which situations conflicts may arise, most OECD countries have tried to define those areas that are most at risk and to provide guidance to prevent and resolve conflict-of-interest situations. Indeed, some public officials operate in sensitive areas with a higher potential risk of conflict of interest, such as justice, tax and customs administrations, as well as the political/administrative interface, and as such, call for the development of special standards. Of respondents to OECD surveys on the subject, 59% have adopted special measures for their ministers and 50% for senior public officials, while staff in ministerial offices, inspectors, and custom officers tend to receive less attention in this regard (Figure 4.1).

Figure 4.1. Development of specific conflict-of-interest policy/rules for particular categories of public officials in OECD countries

Category	Share
Staff in Ministerial cabinet/office	25%
Inspectors at the central level of government	28%
Customs officers	31%
Political advisors/appointees	34%
Tax officials	38%
Auditors	41%
Financial market regulators	41%
Procurement officials	47%
Senior public servants	50%
Ministers	59%

Source: (OECD, 2014[11]).

Thailand has also launched some initiatives to develop specific guidelines for at-risk public officials to manage conflicts of interest. For example, NACC, in consultation with the Ministry of Public Health, has developed manuals for the officials working at the Ministry. Similarly, NACC has set up an *ad hoc* subcommittee to prepare an operation manual for state officials who work in the area of accounting and infrastructure, and has established a working group to analyse the risks of conflict of interest for NACC officials. However, such specific guidelines are still not well developed in other government agencies and areas.

To build on successful initiatives such as the one by NACC and Ministry of Public Heath, PACC could consider consultations with other Ministries and government agencies to help them develop more specific guidelines and codes at organisational levels, while ensuring that they align with the overarching principles integral to the public sector. Furthermore, PACC could encourage each Ministry to elaborate specific conflict-of-interest regulations and guidelines in a participatory fashion. Involving public officials of the organisation in developing such policies is an important awareness-raising exercise, and helps promote a sense of ownership of the policies.

Thailand could consider a mechanism to monitor its cooling-off period, especially for high-ranking public officials and at-risk officials, as well as developing pre-public employment policies

Another area of concern for public sector integrity is conflicts of interest arising from employment before and after the tenure of public officials. Such situations fall under the so-called "revolving-door" phenomenon of mobility between the private and public sectors. On the one hand, it is in the interest of the public and government to attract an experienced and skilled workforce to serve the public interest (OECD, 2015[2]). On the other hand, the revolving door can undermine the integrity of the decision-making process, exposing public officials to the risk of making decisions in the interests of private employers before or after their tenure in public service, rather than in the public interest (OECD, 2015[2]). To avoid conflicts of interest arising before or after public employment, many OECD countries have instituted provisions governing the periods before and after public employment.

In Thailand, a cooling-off period of two years is mandated for all public officials, including state and local officials, the Prime Minister, Ministers and the head of local governments, as stipulated in the Practical Guideline for public officials for Sections 100-103 of the Organic Act on Counter Corruption. While the need for a cooling-off period is clearly stated, there appears to be no mechanism for monitoring and ensuring that public officials follow this rule on leaving their public positions. Several measures can improve the implementation of this mechanism. In terms of institutional responsibility, NACC may continue to be responsible for monitoring the post-public employment of the Prime Minister, Ministers, parliamentarians and other politically appointed or elected officials. However, for other civil servants in the public sector, PACC would be in a better position to conduct the monitoring. For example, before leaving the public sector, public officials who are in a position to become involved in a conflict of interest should have an exit interview with PACC or NACC (depending on the category of public officials) to examine possible conflicts of interest, and, if necessary, to determine the appropriate means of remedying them. In particular, the cooling-off period for senior public officials and at-risk officials should be carefully monitored. Japan, for example, has a Re-employment Surveillance Commission within the Cabinet Office. Civil servants above certain grades must report to the commission on their re-employment status, and the commission updates and publishes the list on its website four times a year.[1] The list includes such information as the name of the public official, the name of the new employer, and the position offered to the public official. PACC, in consultation with NACC, could consider introducing a similar reporting mechanism for public officials to ensure their compliance with cooling-off periods.

To reduce unnecessary administrative burdens, time limits could also be tailored to the level of public officials and specific groups or a particular risk area. For example, in Canada, a one-year time limit is imposed on public officials in executive positions, whereas for ministers, a two-year period is applied (OECD, 2010[3]). In this sense, Thailand might consider conducting consultation with relevant government stakeholders and introducing different durations for cooling-off periods of different categories of officials.

In contrast to post-public employment, there is no explicit restriction on pre-public employment in Thailand. While this is also the case in many OECD countries and requires further efforts to regulate, seven countries – Australia, Austria, France, Israel, Japan, the Netherlands and New Zealand – have restrictions on both private sector employees or lobbyists and suppliers to the government or those who negotiate public sector contracts on behalf of a company when filling a post in the public sector (Figure 4.2).

Figure 4.2. Restrictions on pre-public employment, 2014

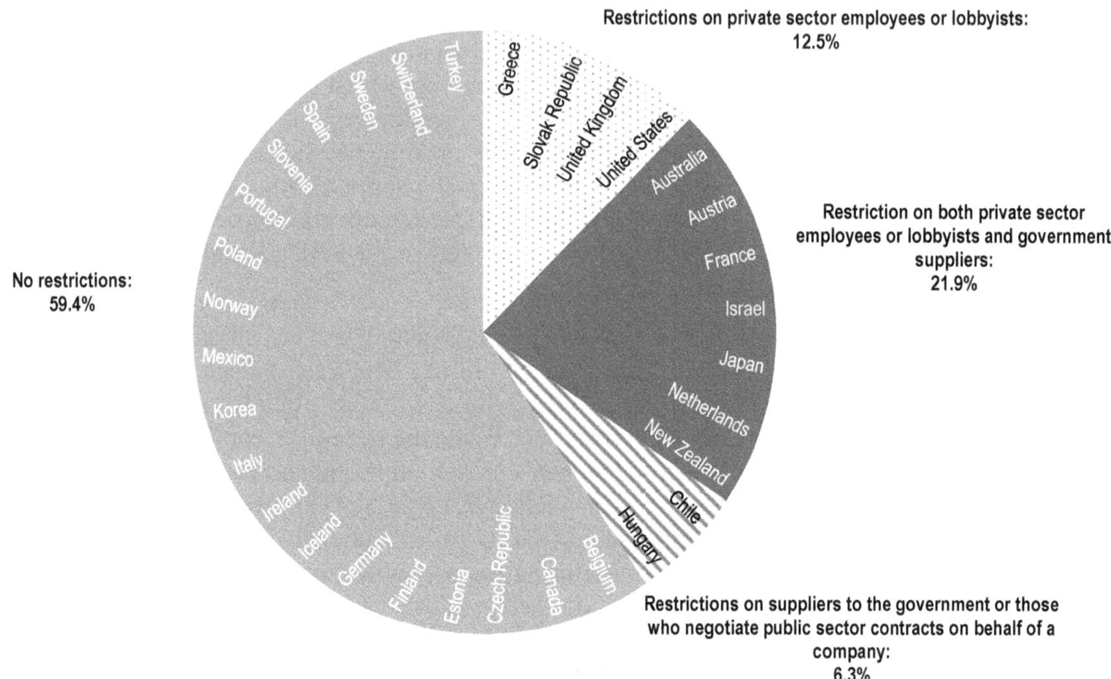

Note: Data unavailable for Denmark and Luxembourg. Government suppliers here could refer to suppliers to the government or those who negotiate public sector contracts on behalf of a company.
Source: (OECD, 2014[1]).

Most restrictions in those countries take place during the recruitment process, when the applicants' previous employment is assessed for potential conflicts of interest. Once recruited, applicants could also be expected to manage their conflicts of interest through recusal from involvement in an affected decision-making process or restriction from certain information (OECD, 2015[2]).

To further safeguard the integrity of public officials and mitigate the risks of conflict of interest, PACC, in consultation with NACC and other government agencies, could consider developing pre-public employment policies in which the applicants' previous employment is assessed for potential conflicts of interest.

Thailand may consider developing a more structured approach to raise awareness of conflicts of interest

The previous chapter on public ethics touched upon the value of developing practical guidelines and examples of ethical dilemmas and conflict-of-interest situations. Without communication and proactive dissemination, however, values remain words on paper. The vast majority of OECD member countries have measures to systematically distribute and communicate the need for managing conflicts of interest for public servants.

In Thailand, some public agencies provide rules on conflict of interest as part of an introductory package for newly recruited staff, as well as *ad hoc* training courses on the subject. NACC is also invited to other government agencies to discuss and raise awareness on managing conflicts of interest. NACC recently spoke about the management of conflict of interest at the Ministry of Industry, for example. However, these awareness-raising initiatives are not integrated into formal conflict-of-interest management policies.

In consultation with NACC, PACC and Anti-Corruption Operation Centres, and to increase understanding of managing conflicts of interest in the public sector and ensure co-ordination across the government, each government agency might consider developing systematic procedures in which training, education and guidance on management of conflicts of interest are provided to all public officials at different stages of their career. The most frequently used method in OECD countries is to provide the guidelines whenever new recruits are admitted to the public service (Table 4.1). PACC might also consider formally requiring government agencies to disseminate manuals on management of conflict of interest on hiring new staff, and providing training on the subject on a regular basis.

Table 4.1. Awareness-raising activities for managing conflict of interest

	Initial dissemination of rules/guidelines to public officials upon taking office	Proactive updates regarding changes in conflict-of-interest rules/guidelines	Publication of the conflict-of-interest policy online or on the intranet of the organisation	Regular reminders as to what a conflict of interest is, and the responsibility of public officials to resolve them	Provision of training	Provision of regular guidance and assistance	Providing an advice line or help desk where officials receive guidance on filing requirements or identify or manage conflicts of interest
Australia	●	●	●	●	●	●	●
Austria	●	●	○	●	●	●	○
Belgium	●	○	●	●	●	●	●
Canada	●	●	●	●	●	●	●
Chile	●	○	●	○	●	●	○
Czech Republic	○	○	○	○	○	○	○
Estonia	○	●	●	○	●	●	●
Finland	●	○	●	○	●	○	○

	Initial dissemination of rules/guidelines to public officials upon taking office	Proactive updates regarding changes in conflict-of-interest rules/guidelines	Publication of the conflict-of-interest policy online or on the intranet of the organisation	Regular reminders as to what a conflict of interest is, and the responsibility of public officials to resolve them	Provision of training	Provision of regular guidance and assistance	Providing an advice line or help desk where officials receive guidance on filing requirements or identify or manage conflicts of interest
France	○	○	○	●	●	○	●
Germany	●	●	●	●	●	●	●
Greece	●	●	●	○	○	○	○
Hungary	●	●	○	○	○	○	●
Iceland	●	●	●	●	●	●	○
Ireland	●	●	●	○	○	○	●
Israel	●	○	○	○	○	●	○
Italy	○	○	●	●	○	●	○
Japan	●	●	●	○	●	○	○
Korea	●	○	●	●	●	●	●
Mexico	●	●	○	○	○	○	○
Netherlands	●	●	●	●	●	●	●
New Zealand	●	●	●	●	●	●	●
Norway	●	●	●	○	●	●	●
Poland	●	○	●	○	○	●	○
Portugal	●	○	○	●	●	○	○
Slovak Republic	○	○	○	○	○	○	○
Slovenia	●	○	○	○	●	●	●
Spain	●	●	●	●	●	●	●
Sweden	●	●	●	●	●	○	○
Switzerland	●	●	●	●	●	●	●
Turkey	●	○	○	○	●	○	○
United Kingdom	●	●	●	●	●	●	●
United States	●	●	●	●	●	●	●
Yes ●	27	19	22	17	23	20	17
No ○	5	13	11	15	9	12	15

Source: (OECD, 2014[1]).

When there is a limited budget or resources for awareness-raising programmes, it is crucial to prioritise the target groups. Targeting also helps to focus the awareness-raising activities on the practical needs of a specific group of public officials, increasing their motivation to observe the rules. Several groups could be targeted for training on managing conflicts of interest: all new public officials; elected public officials, senior public officials in management positions and public officials in areas of risk. Compulsory training for these groups is advisable. In addition, officers in each Anti-Corruption Operation Centre could be trained for their role in dissemination and advice on conflict-of-interest policies in the organisation.

Thailand could consider developing a mechanism to monitor the effectiveness of conflict-of-interest policies

An emerging issue for many countries is to monitor and assess the effectiveness of the existing conflict-of-interest policies. In Thailand, no major research has been initiated to determine how familiar public officials are with conflict-of-interest policies. The absence of measurements related to the degree of familiarisation with the principles and values makes it difficult to monitor whether the conflict-of-interest policies are implemented and respected. As a first step, PACC, in consultation and co-operation with NACC, could consider reviewing how public organisations provide guidance on the conflict of interest policies, reviewing public employees' knowledge of such policies, and monitoring implementation of the policies through such diagnostic tools as surveys and statistical data. Countries such as Australia, Canada, Estonia, Korea, New Zealand, Portugal and the United States use employee feedback mechanisms and other specific tools for assessing their policy implementation on a regular basis (Box 4.3).

Box 4.3. Monitoring of the conflict of interest programme in the United States

The Unites States Office of Government Ethics (OGE) comprehensively monitors implementation of the executive branch conflict-of-interest programme. OGE employs several means, including surveys, diagnostic tools, training and outreach, to prevent and resolve conflicts of interest. Over 130 executive branch agencies are required to submit an annual survey report to OGE concerning conflict of interest and other aspects of their ethics programmes. Responses are mandatory and provide OGE with compliance metrics to assess the effectiveness of each agency's conflict-of-interest programme. OGE also surveys ethics officials annually to assess the effectiveness of OGE's guidance, training and support concerning conflicts of interest.

Source: OECD Survey on Management of Conflict of Interest (2012).

Thailand could consider introducing an asset disclosure system for senior public officials and other officials at risk

Disclosure of the private interests of public officials is an effective tool for preventing illicit enrichment. Implementing rules that public officials must disclose their assets at the start of their tenure, midway through their tenure and at the end of their tenure can help the relevant authorities ensure that public officials are not using their position for personal gain. Furthermore, although it is primarily public officials' responsibility to manage their conflicts of interest, disclosure of their private interests can greatly help prevent potential instances of conflict of interest.

In Thailand, the Constitution of the Kingdom of Thailand, B.E. 2560, requires persons holding political positions, judges of the Constitutional Court, persons holding positions in independent organs, the Auditor-General and state officials to submit an account showing to the NACC particulars of their assets and liabilities, of their spouses and children who have not yet become *sui juris*, in accordance with the Organic Act on Anti-Corruption. Sections 39-42 of the Organic Act on Counter Corruption, B.E. 2542, provide provisions that state officials make a declaration of the assets and liabilities. The Act requires high-ranking public officials, including the President of the Supreme Court of Justice, the President of the Constitutional Court, the President of the Supreme Administrative Court, the Prosecutor-General, the Election Commissioner and Ombudsman to disclose their assets and liabilities and those of their spouses and dependent children upon taking office, every three years while they are in office and on vacating office.[2] In addition, public officials at the PACC are required to submit an asset declaration form to the Secretary-General of the PACC.

NACC recently issued a new notification expanding the scope of the asset disclosure under the Organic Act on Counter Corruption, B.E. 2542.[3] Under this new initiative, which came into force on 4 January 2017, the scope was further extended to include public officials such as NACC senior officials, Presidents of the Appeals Court, and sub-national senior public officials, including the Deputy Permanent Secretary of the Bangkok Metropolitan Administration (BMA). In addition, the NACC Notification (No.5), B.E.2560, requires that 50 additional state official positions submit their assets and liabilities, including the Vice-President of Public Universities, the Municipal Clerk, and Deputy Commissioner of the National Police.

Such an initiative is an encouraging sign. However, since senior public officials at other ministries and at-risk public officials such as procurement officials are also exposed to corruption, NACC could consider introducing an asset disclosure system for senior public officials and other at-risk officials. In Japan, asset disclosure is mandatory for all public officials at the rank of Deputy Director General or above at the headquarters of all government agencies (Box 4.4).

Box 4.4. Reviews of asset disclosure forms in Japan

The Ethics Act of Japan stipulates three types of mandatory reporting systems (see below), to promote a transparent relationship between national public employees and other stakeholders. The National Public Service Ethics Board examines copies of the reports sent from each ministry.

Types of reports

1. Mandatory reports on the receipt of gifts (to be submitted by the officials at the rank of Assistant Director and above at the headquarters; when they accept gifts, food and drink, remuneration for a lecture and other activities, and any other benefits from business counterparts which exceeds JPY 5 000, approximately EUR 36).
2. Mandatory reports on the exchange of stocks (to be submitted by the officials at the rank of Deputy Director General or above at the headquarters).
3. Mandatory reports on income (to be submitted by the officials at the rank of Deputy Director General or above at the headquarters).

Report procedure

Asset disclosure mechanism in Japan

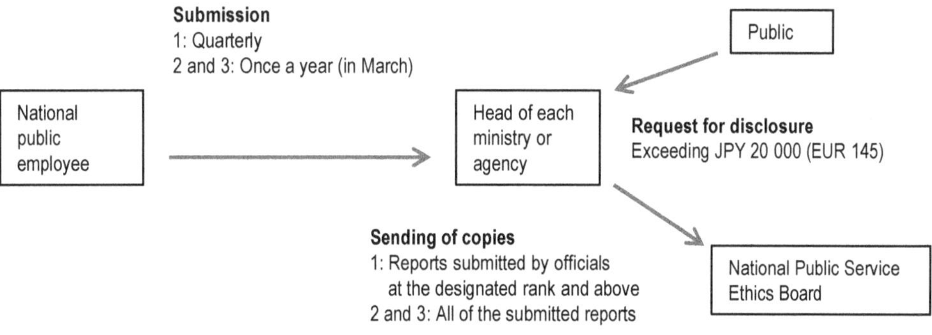

Source: National Public Service Ethics Board, www.jinji.go.jp/rinri/eng/index.htm.

Thailand could consider making asset disclosure forms publicly accessible for scrutiny by the media and the citizens

Beyond the scope of the declaration, it is also essential to establish a system of oversight to provide monitoring and enforcement. The effectiveness of the disclosure regime depends on the system's ability to detect violations and administer sanctions. In Thailand, disclosure forms are only subject to internal audit by the NACC. In this regard, publicly disclosing asset disclosure forms might add an extra layer of monitoring, allowing citizens themselves to scrutinise the information submitted.

In Thailand, the Organic Act on Counter Corruption (No. 2), B.E. 2544, stipulates that the assets and liabilities of persons holding the position of Prime Minister, Minister, Member of the House of Representatives and Senator can be disclosed to the public, while other positions are not disclosed mandatorily. Disclosed documents are kept at the Office of the NACC for the public and media for inspection during office hours, and are made available on the NACC website. Applying a wider publication policy to high-ranking civil servants will increase the level of accountability and transparency. Making such information public will also allow public scrutiny and help increase integrity in the public sector. Information relating to private interests of public officials may also be published on the government portal website managed by the Electronic Government Agency.

In OECD countries, the level of disclosure, on average, is closely related to the level of seniority. Disclosure requirements for top decision makers are the most extensive, followed by senior civil servants, political advisors or appointees and civil servants (Figure 4.3). Reflecting on this global trend, NACC could consider expanding the level of disclosure, to ensure transparency and the accountability of public officials.

Figure 4.3. Level of disclosure and public availability of private interests within the executive branch

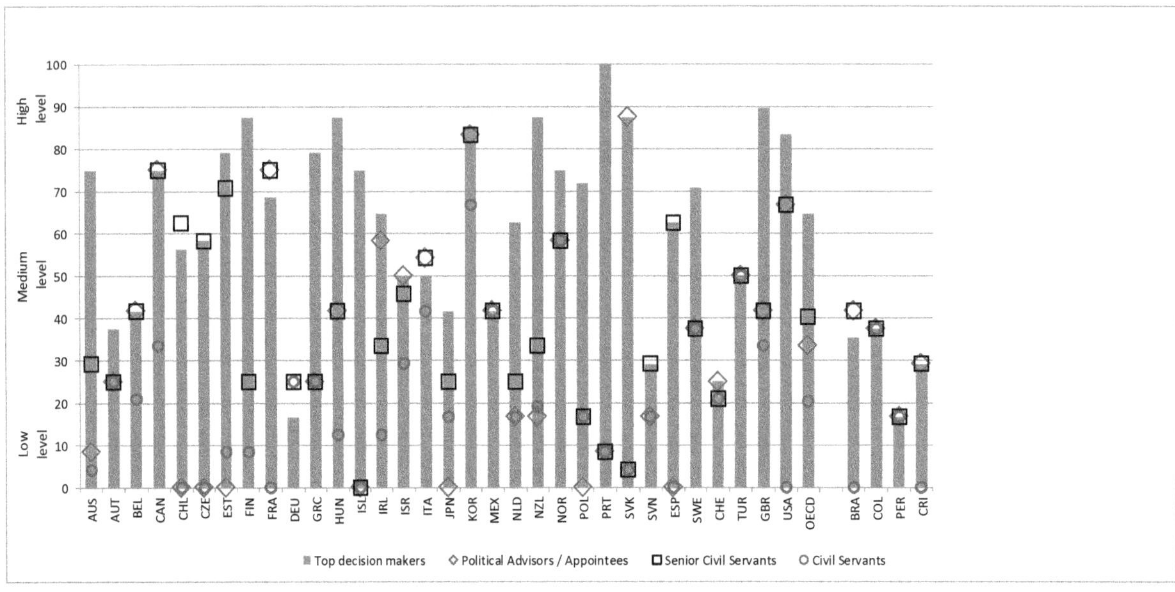

Source: (OECD, 2014[1]).

Thailand could consider developing an online management system of asset disclosure, to facilitate reviewing, auditing and publication by the NACC

Because the number of public officials subject to asset disclosure has recently increased, the capacity of NACC to audit and verify these asset disclosure forms needs to be increased. One way to strengthen the auditing capacity of NACC is to invest in online technologies and introduce an online management system of asset disclosure.

Asset declarations in Thailand are now paper-based, but the development of an online system is under discussion. For example, introduction of an online asset declaration system for legislators and high-ranking public officials was proposed to the National Reform Council in 2014. This initiative should be encouraged, and NACC could consider introducing a comprehensive online disclosure system to promote transparency in the public sector.

Such a reform plan could benefit from online management of asset disclosure (Box 4.5). This would make asset disclosure a simpler process for those filing and facilitate data collection for the NACC. It is easier to collect data in this way rather than reading handwritten forms and to spend time recording the information, potentially introducing inaccuracies. It is also easier for filers to have a consistent, online, easy-to-access interface for submitting information. Online technology also makes it easier to organise the information in an intelligible, user-friendly way that facilitates reviewing, auditing and subsequent publication (U4 Anti-Corruption Resource Centre, 2015[4]).

Box 4.5. Some potential benefits of online asset disclosure identified by the U4 Anti-Corruption Resource Centre

- Technology makes it possible to automate complete and consistent information, reducing delays caused by incomplete or incorrect declarations. Online submission systems can prevent many mistakes, providing guidance to the filers on how to file the information, and alerting them to missing, incomplete or erroneous entries. Electronic filing also allows for standardisation of a wide range of terms and financial terminology that can be used differently by filers using "drop-down" menus.
- Electronic filing may save time for both filers and agency staff. Online submission may increase compliance by reducing the filers' time and the cost of physically submitting their declaration, while eliminating for agency staff the cumbersome process of transferring data from paper to electronic data management systems.
- Electronic submission facilitates compliance checks verifying whether officials have submitted their declarations within the required deadlines. Statistical information and overall analysis of all declarations is easy to implement.
- Electronic declarations facilitate the management and retrieval of data, allowing declarations to be retained, consulted and compared more easily for longer periods of time, as opposed to archiving and locating physical copies.
- Software can automatically calculate and flag numerical imbalances and identify suspicious patterns, facilitating verification. Electronic filing also makes it easier to cross-check declared information with other databases or to share the information with other state agencies, such as prosecution services and financial intelligence units.

Source: (U4 Anti-Corruption Resource Centre, 2015[4]).

After Indonesia introduced an online management system in 2001, the compliance rate increased from 56% in 2006 to 85% in 2009, facilitating verification of the forms by the Corruption Eradication Commission (KPK) (Box 4.6). Similarly, the introduction of technology in Argentina had a significant impact on the effectiveness of the asset declaration scheme. In the year following implementation of the automated submission system, submission compliance rates increased from 67% to 96%, and the estimated cost to the government per declaration decreased from USD 70 to USD 8. The number of conflict-of-interest investigations increased from 40 to 331, and the number of financial disclosure information requests increased from 66 to 823 (The World Bank, 2013[5]).

Box 4.6. Online management system of asset disclosure in Indonesia

An asset declaration mechanism was introduced in Indonesia in 2001 and is managed by the Corruption Eradication Commission (KPK). Declarations are submitted on paper, but administrative and operational data management processes are online. The declarations are submitted in hard copy (about 116 500 in 2009), and scanned for archival and retrieval purposes. The data is then processed by about 80 staff, and line managers help to validate the data. A sample of 1% to 5% of declarations is verified, primarily targeting the declarations of officials in high-risk agencies, selected manually by cross-checking various KPK databases. The KPK has introduced enhanced analysis and reporting, using data warehouse and business intelligence tools that provide increased verification options and the publication of statistics and trends.

Summaries of wealth disclosure reports are published in the state gazette and online. The portal provides public access to compliance statistics and other reports evaluating the system's performance. A user can search and analyse the data based on a number of factors, such as name, gender, job title and property data, and print reports (The World Bank, 2013[5]).

The KPK provides guidance to filers on completing a declaration both through its website (www.kpk.go.id) and in person at the KPK. Officials can also make an appointment at the KPK for this purpose.

Source: (U4 Anti-Corruption Resource Centre, 2015[4]) and (The World Bank, 2013[5]).

In developing an online management system, Thailand would need to pay attention to the interconnectivity of such systems across different government agencies. Experience in other countries suggests that a failure to develop compatible platforms and software systems can impede the efficient exchange between government agencies of of data that is needed to expose corruption and successfully prosecute corruption cases. In particular, the online platform and software for asset disclosure must be compatible with that of relevant agencies, such as prosecutorial agencies (U4 Anti-Corruption Resource Centre, 2015[4]).

Proposals for action

- Thailand could consider consolidating the mandate for public sector integrity. PACC could be designated as the agency responsible for conflict-of-interest policies for civil servants in the public sector, in close co-operation with NACC.
- Thailand could consider developing specific guidance for categories of public officials who are at risk due to the nature of their work. With support from PACC, each government agency could consider providing more specific guidelines and codes at organisational levels, while ensuring that they align with the overarching principles integral to the public sector. In addition, PACC could encourage government agencies to elaborate such specific conflict-of-interest regulations and guidelines in a participatory fashion.
- Thailand could consider introducing a mechanism to monitor the implementation of its cooling-off period, especially for high-ranking public officials and at-risk officials, as well as developing pre-public employment policies. While there is a cooling-off period of two years for all public officials including the Prime Minister, Ministers and the heads of local governments, no mechanism exists to monitor and ensure that public officials follow this rule upon leaving their public positions. NACC and PACC could consider developing measures to monitor the implementation of the cooling-off period, and also develop pre-public employment policies.
- Thailand might consider developing a more structured approach to raise awareness of conflicts of interest. PACC and the Anti-Corruption Operation Centre in each government agency may consider developing more systematic procedures, in which training, education and guidance on management of conflicts of interest are provided to all public officials throughout their career.
- Thailand could consider developing a mechanism to monitor the effectiveness of the conflict-of-interest policies. PACC could consider reviewing how public organisations provide guidance on the conflict-of-interest policies, assessing public employees' knowledge of such policies, and monitoring the implementation of the policies through diagnostic tools such as surveys and statistical data.
- Thailand could consider extending an asset disclosure system to senior public officials and other at-risk officials, while increasing the NACC's auditing capacity.
- Thailand could consider making asset disclosure forms publicly accessible for scrutiny by the media and the citizens in a gradual and progressive manner, taking into account the level and position of the public official. Information relating to private interests of public officials could be published on the government portal website managed by the Electronic Government Agency.
- Thailand could consider introducing a comprehensive online disclosure system to facilitate effective reviewing, auditing and subsequent publication by the NACC. In developing an online management system, Thailand would also need to pay attention to interconnectivity of such systems across different government agencies.

Notes

[1] www.cas.go.jp/jp/gaiyou/jimu/jinjikyoku/files/kouhyou_h2907041_siryou.pdf.

[2] https://www.nacc.go.th/ewt_news.php?nid=953.

[3] Notification regarding specific positions that should submit assets and liabilities for inspection under the Organic Act on Counter Corruption, B.E. 2542 (1999), and under Section 40, amended by the Organic Act on Counter Corruption (No. 2), B.E. 2554 (2011), (No. 4), B.E. 2559 (2016).

References

OECD (2010), *Post-Public Employment: Good Practices for Preventing Conflict of Interest*, OECD Publishing, Paris, http://dx.doi.org/10.1787/9789264056701-en. [3]

OECD (2014), *OECD Survey on Managing Conflict of Interest in the Executive Branch and Whistleblower Protection*, http://www.oecd.org/gov/ethics/2014-survey-managing-conflict-of-interest.pdf (accessed on 14 February 2018). [1]

OECD (2015), *Government at a Glance 2015*, OECD Publishing, Paris, http://dx.doi.org/10.1787/gov_glance-2015-en. [2]

The World Bank (2013), "Income and Asset Disclosure: Case Study Illustrations", *Directions in Development, Washington, DC*, http://dx.doi.org/10.1596/978-0-8213-9796-1. [5]

U4 Anti-Corruption Resource Centre (2015), *The use of technology for managing income and asset declarations*, http://www.u4.no/publications/the-use-of-technology-for-managing-income-and-asset-declarations/. [4]

Chapter 5. Encouraging reporting of corruption in Thailand through stronger whistleblower protection

While provisions for whistleblower protection are cursorily mentioned in the Executive Measures in Anti-Corruption Act, B.E. 2551, and Penalty in Witness Protection Act, B.E. 2546, Thailand has no dedicated whistleblower protection law. To develop a stronger whistleblower protection mechanism to improve integrity in the public sector, this chapter discusses the value of developing legislation to address the issue of whistleblowing, suggesting a number of key features that need to be included, such as clear definition of wrongdoing and retaliation, multiple reporting channels, remedies for whistleblowers and monitoring of the law's implementation, with reference to good practices of OECD countries.

The statistical data for Israel are supplied by and under the responsibility of the relevant Israeli authorities. The use of such data by the OECD is without prejudice to the status of the Golan Heights, East Jerusalem and Israeli settlements in the West Bank under the terms of international law.

Encouraging integrity and an open organisational culture by detection and protection

Effective mechanisms for disclosing wrongdoing without fear of reprisal are at the heart of integrity in government. The protection of employees who disclose wrongdoing in the workplace ("whistleblowers") is thus an essential part of an organisation's system of promoting a culture of public accountability. In many countries, protecting whistleblowers is proving to be a crucial element in the reporting of misconduct, fraud and corruption. Employees who report wrongdoing may be subject to intimidation, harassment, dismissal and violence by their colleagues or superiors. In many countries, whistleblowing is even associated with treason or spying (Banisar, 2011[1]; Transparency International, 2009[2]). This may be the result of prevailing cultural conventions, which may also shape individual careers and internal organisational culture (Latimer and Brown, 2008[3]). Provisions that encourage whistleblowers to come forward must be set up, including: legal protection from retaliation, clear guidance on reporting procedures, and visible support and positive reinforcement from the organisational hierarchy.

Well-designed whistleblower frameworks in OECD countries clearly define the kind of wrongdoing that justifies protection and which provides both internal and external confidential channels for disclosing misconduct. Dedicated recipients are made accountable for ensuring the confidentiality of the whistleblower's identity and of the information communicated, as well as how they act upon such disclosures. Good practices in OECD countries often provide appropriate remedies that correct and compensate for the reprisals that ensue as a result of whistleblowers' disclosure of misconduct.

Thailand could consider developing a dedicated law to protect whistleblowers, in addition to existing witness protection arrangements

Thailand has no dedicated whistleblower protection legislation. The issue is partially covered by the Executive Measures in Anti-Corruption Act, B.E. 2551, and the Penalty in Witness Protection Act, B.E. 2546. Section 57 of the Executive Measures in Anti-Corruption Act, B.E. 2551, states that if the Office of Public Sector Anti-Corruption Commission (PACC) considers that whistleblowers are treated unfairly as a result of making a disclosure, PACC shall forward the matter to the Prime Minister who may consider instructing PACC on appropriate measures to protect them (Box 5.1). In addition, Section 103/2-103/5 of the Organic Act on Counter Corruption, B.E. 2542, and its amendment prescribe measures for protecting the person giving testimony or for whistleblowers. Such a person shall be deemed a witness entitled to protection under the laws on witness protection, along with the Regulation of the NACC Witness Protection, B.E. 2554, which prescribes the rules, procedures and conditions of witness protection in cases of corruption, unusual wealth and the inspection of assets and liabilities.

Box 5.1. Section 57 of the Executive Measures in Anti-Corruption Act, B.E. 2551

Section 57: In the case that the persons under Section 53 are State Officials, when the above-mentioned persons file an application with PACC, if such persons continue to perform their duties under the existing affiliations, such person may be retaliated against out of spite or unfairly treated, resulting from alleging or making statements, or giving clues or information, and PACC has considered and is of the opinion that there are grounds to believe that there may be above-mentioned grounds, PACC shall forward this matter to the Prime Minister for consideration, to instruct that the aforesaid persons be protected or whether there shall be any other measures to protect the aforesaid persons as the Prime Minister thinks fit.

Source: Executive Measures in Anti-Corruption Act, B.E. 2551.

These provisions currently lack such details as the definition of state officials and unfair treatments, the criteria upon which PACC should forward the case to the Prime Minister, and remedies for whistleblowers. Unclear boundaries and distinctions that are not explicitly explained can create confusion and a lack of confidence in the protection system, so that as a result, few whistleblowers may come forward to report wrongdoing.

In addition, the Executive Measures in Anti-Corruption Act, B.E. 2551, does not make a clear distinction between witness protection and whistleblower protection. Interviews with PACC officials also indicated that many public officials assume that the existing witness protection mechanism also covers whistleblowers, and that protective measures under witness protection may be sufficient for whistleblowers. Section 53 states that protective measures may be provided to the person making the allegation, the injured person, the filer of a motion or complaint, and the accuser, maker of a statement or anyone who gives any information in association with corruption in the public sector. Section 54 then states that in criminal cases, protective measures shall be provided to those defined by Section 53 under the laws on witness protection. The Regulation of the NACC Witness Protection, B.E. 2554, also has some provisions for witness protection in corruption cases. Legally speaking, some overlap is typical between whistleblowers and witnesses, because some whistleblowers may possess solid evidence and eventually become witnesses in legal proceedings (Transparency International, 2013[4]). When whistleblowers testify during court proceedings, they can be covered under witness protection laws. However, if the subject matter of a whistleblower report does not result in criminal proceedings, or if the whistleblower is never called as a witness, no witness protection is provided.

Given that whistleblowers are usually employees of the organisation where the reported misconduct took place, they may face specific risks that are not currently covered by the witness protection laws, such as demotion or dismissal. Whistleblowers may be retaliated against and lose their position because they may not be able to return to their workplace for personal and professional reasons. They can find themselves unemployed for a long period as a result of being ostracised from their professional community and network and potentially blacklisted from future employment within their field of work. In this regard, the typical measures provided under the witness protection law, such as relocation, police protection and changed identity, may not always be relevant in the case of whistleblowers.

To reinforce the provision underpinned by Section 57 of the Executive Measures in Anti-Corruption Act, B.E. 2551, and make a clear distinction between witness protection and whistleblower protection, Thailand could consider developing a dedicated whistleblower law, assigning to PACC responsibility for the implementation of such a law. Whistleblower protection can originate in a single dedicated law, or through a piecemeal approach stemming from provisions in various laws. Dedicated legislation is the preferable option, because the degree of protection afforded within the provisions of various laws tends to be less comprehensive. Protection provided for under dedicated legislation can provide clarity and help streamline processes and mechanisms involved in disclosing wrongdoing.

For this reason, dedicated whistleblower protection laws are coming into force in a growing number of OECD countries. Over the last decade, an increasing number of OECD countries have developed a specific legal framework to protect whistleblowers. OECD countries have established more dedicated whistleblower protection laws in the past five years than in the previous quarter-century (Figure 5.1).

Figure 5.1. Entry into force of dedicated whistleblower protection laws: A timeline

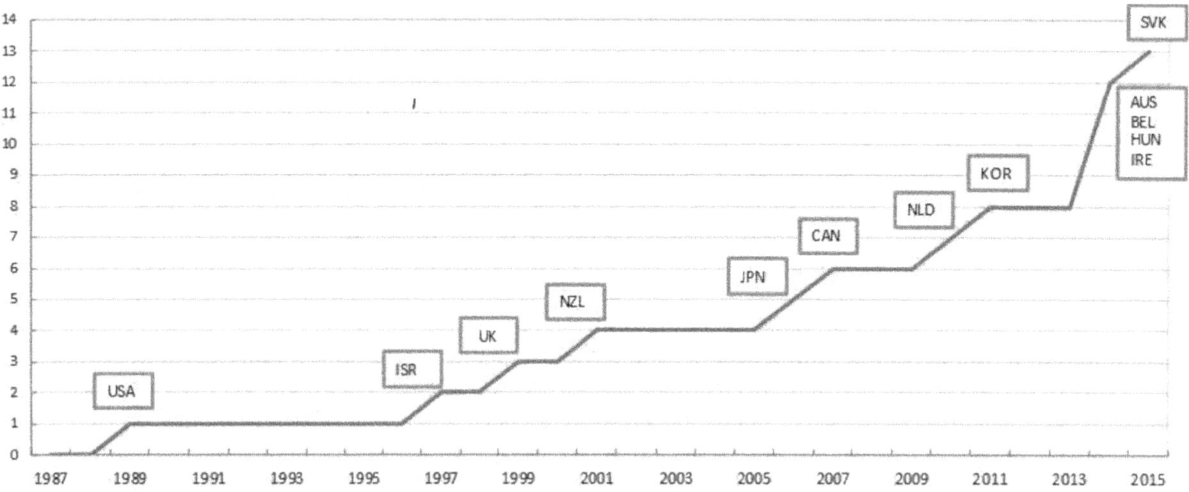

Source: (OECD, 2016[5]).

Thailand could consider developing a broader definition of whistleblowers

As a first step in developing a comprehensive whistleblower protection mechanism in Thailand, introducing a broader interpretation of the term whistleblower would make it possible to offer protection to a larger number of individuals. It is vital for Thailand to ensure that the coverage afforded to whistleblowers follows a "no loophole" approach, meaning that in addition to public officials and permanent employees in the private sector, specific categories of employees, often in grey areas, are explicitly designated as qualifying for protection. Such employees, for instance, should include those outside the traditional employee-employer relationship (e.g. consultants, contractors, trainees/interns, temporary employees, former employees and volunteers). In cases of public sector whistleblower protection provisions, a "no loophole" approach would signify that employees of state-owned or -controlled enterprises and statutory agencies also qualify for protection. While there are varying degrees of whistleblower protection in the public sector across 26 OECD member countries (Table 5.1), many countries opt for providing protection to former employees, consultants and also temporary employees.

Table 5.1. Varying degrees of whistleblower protection in the public sector

	Employees	Consultants	Suppliers	Temporary employees	Former employees
Australia	●	●	●	●	●
Austria	●	○	○	●	●
Belgium	●	○	○	●	○
Canada	●	●	●	●	●
Chile	●	○	○	○	○
Estonia	●	●	●	●	●
France	●	●	●	●	●
Germany	●	●	●	●	●
Hungary	●	●	●	●	●
Iceland	●	○	○	●	○
Ireland	●	●	●	●	●
Israel	●	●	○	●	●
Italy	●	●	○	●	●
Japan	●	○	○	●	○
Korea	●	●	●	●	●
Mexico	●	●	●	●	●
Netherlands	●	○	○	●	●
New Zealand	●	●	●	●	●
Norway	●	○	○	○	○
Portugal	●	●	●	●	●
Slovak Republic	●	○	○	○	○
Slovenia	●	●	●	●	●
Switzerland	●	○	○	●	○

	Employees	Consultants	Suppliers	Temporary employees	Former employees
Turkey	●	●	❍	●	❍
United Kingdom	●	●	●	●	❍
United States	●	●	❍	●	●
Total OECD 26					
Yes: ●	26	17	13	23	17
No: ❍	0	9	13	3	9

Source: (OECD, 2016[5]).

Thailand could consider establishing a clear definition of the scope of disclosures that justify coverage under the whistleblower protection system

Another vital element for an effective whistleblower protection law is the precise classification of elements of disclosure that warrant protection. In Thailand, Section 53 of the Executive Measures in Anti-Corruption Act, B.E. 2551, specifies that protection is offered to those who disclose information on corruption in the public sector. While the provision of protection for whistleblowers who disclose acts of corruption is a key element of an effective whistleblower framework, disclosures of other types of wrongdoing should also be included (Figure 5.2). Individuals who witness or are aware of other types of wrongdoing, such as violations of the code of conduct or conflict-of-interest policies, gross waste or mismanagement, etc., could feel free to come forward to to the relevant authorities. Together, this would encourage the prevention not only of corruption in the public service, but of wrongdoing more generally.

Figure 5.2. Percentage of surveyed OECD countries providing protection for disclosure of specific categories of misconduct

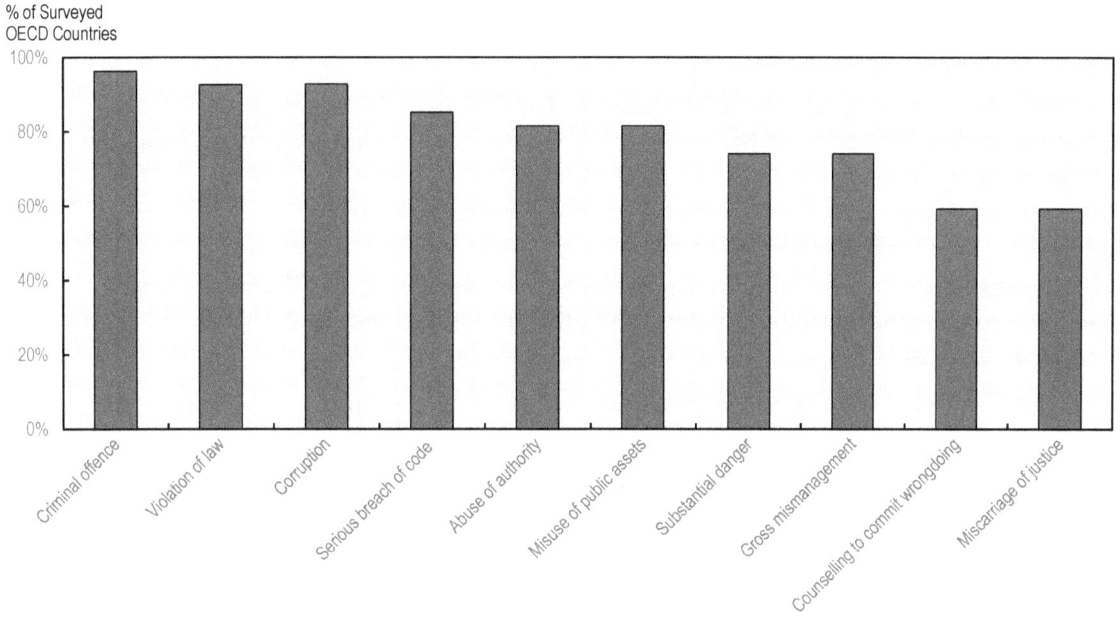

% of Surveyed OECD Countries
100%
80%
60%
40%
20%
0%
Criminal offence
Violation of law
Corruption
Serious breach of code
Abuse of authority
Misuse of public assets
Substantial danger
Gross mismanagement
Counselling to commit wrongdoing
Miscarriage of justice

Note: Respondents were asked the following question: "Which of the following wrongdoing constitutes a protected disclosure?"
Source: (OECD, 2014[35]).

In addition, PACC could consider establishing a clear definition of the scope of wrongdoing that could warrant coverage under the law. The lack of clarity can undermine the confidence that whistleblowers may have in bringing forward information about potential instances of corruption. To mitigate the likelihood of having whistleblowers come forward with information that may not qualify as protected disclosures, potentially exposing them to unnecessary risks and overburdening the intake system with non-applicable cases, PACC may wish to consider providing a detailed and balanced definition of potential wrongdoing. Establishing a clear classification of wrongdoing will also avoid situations where PACC and the officers responsible take the liberty of establishing their own definition of wrongdoings, which can lead to abuse, lack of consistency and much uncertainty as to whether protection will be granted from one case to the next.

The ideal balance should encourage reporting on a range of potential wrongdoing, without being so detailed that potential whistleblowers are not sure whether they would be afforded protection for disclosure of a particular wrongdoing. For example, the UK legislation provides a balanced approach, with a detailed definition, and spells out exceptions (Box 5.2).

Box 5.2. A detailed definition of protected disclosures in the United Kingdom

Part IV – A: Protected disclosure

43A: Meaning of "protected disclosure"

In this Act a "protected disclosure" means a qualifying disclosure (as defined by Section 43B, which is made by a worker in accordance with any of Sections 43C to 43H.

43B: Disclosures qualifying for protection

(1) In this Part, a "qualifying disclosure" means any disclosure of information which, in the reasonable belief of the worker making the disclosure, tends to show one or more of the following:

(a) that a criminal offence has been committed, is being committed or is likely to be committed,

(b) that a person has failed, is failing or is likely to fail to comply with any legal obligation to which he is subject,

(c) that a miscarriage of justice has occurred, is occurring or is likely to occur,

(d) that the health or safety of any individual has been, is being or is likely to be endangered,

(e) that the environment has been, is being or is likely to be damaged, or

(f) that information tending to show any matter falling within any one of the preceding paragraphs has been, is being or is likely to be deliberately concealed.

(2) For the purposes of Subsection (1), it is immaterial whether the relevant failure occurred, occurs or would occur in the United Kingdom or elsewhere, and whether the law applying to it is that of the United Kingdom or of any other country or territory.

(3) A disclosure of information is not a qualifying disclosure if the person making the disclosure commits an offence by making it.

(4) A disclosure of information in respect of which a claim to legal professional privilege (or, in Scotland, to confidentiality as between client and professional legal adviser) could be maintained in legal proceedings is not a qualifying disclosure if it is made by a person to whom the information had been disclosed in the course of obtaining legal advice.

(5) In this Part, "the relevant failure", in relation to a qualifying disclosure, means the matter falling within Paragraphs (a) to (f) of Subsection (1).

Source: UK Public Disclosure Act of 1998, Part IV-A to Employment Rights Act of 1996.

Thailand could establish a comprehensive overview of the types of retaliation against whistleblowers

To protect whistleblowers from reprisals, some countries have specified in their whistleblower protection laws the types of reprisals that are prohibited (Figure 5.3). In most surveyed OECD countries, retaliation such as dismissal, suspension or demotion, transfer or reassignment, change in duties, and decrease of pay benefits, awards or training are specified and considered unlawful in their whistleblower protection laws.

In Thailand, the existing law does not specify the types of retaliation against whistleblowers that are considered unlawful. While Section 57 of the Executive Measures in Anti-Corruption Act, B.E. 2551, makes a reference to the protection of whistleblowers against "unfair treatment", this provision does not provide a clear definition of such treatment. When drafting a new dedicated whistleblower protection law, PACC could consider specifying the types and risks of retaliation against whistleblowers so that protection from prospective professional marginalisation can be mitigated.

Figure 5.3. Percentage of the OECD countries surveyed providing protective measures for each category of reprisals

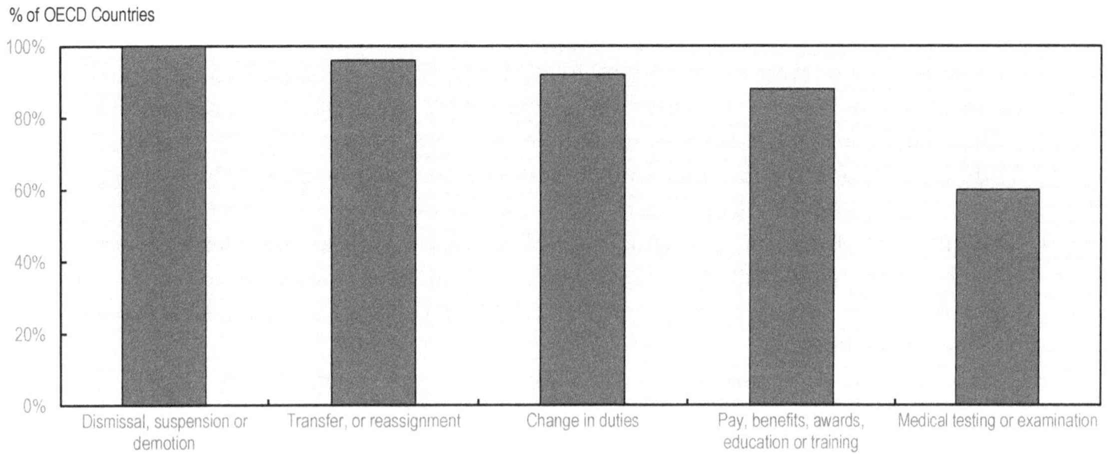

Source: (OECD, 2014[35]).

As a concrete example, the law in Korea (Box 5.3) gives a comprehensive overview of the types of retaliation against whistleblowers that is considered unlawful. Moreover, threatening to take action can have the same effect on the whistleblower as actual retaliation. In Australia's whistleblower protection system, it is not only an offence to undertake an act of reprisal, but also to threaten to undertake an act of reprisal against a person for having made a public interest disclosure.

Box 5.3. Comprehensive list of types of retaliation against whistleblowers in Korea

The term "disadvantageous measures" means an action that falls under any of the following items:

- Removal from office, release from office, dismissal or any other unfavourable personnel action equivalent to the loss of status at work;
- Disciplinary action, suspension from office, reduction in pay, demotion, restriction on promotion and any other unfair personnel actions;
- Work reassignment, transfer, denial of duties, rearrangement of duties or any other personnel actions that are against the whistleblower's will;
- Discrimination in performance evaluation, peer review, etc., and subsequent discrimination in the payment of wages, bonuses, etc.;
- The cancellation of education, training or other self-development opportunities; the restriction or removal of budget, workforce or other available resources, the suspension of access to security information or classified information; the cancellation of authorisation to handle security information or classified information; or any other discrimination or measure detrimental to the working conditions of the whistleblower;
- Putting the whistleblower's name on a black list, as well as the release such a blacklist, bullying, the use of violence and abusive language toward the whistleblower, or any other action that causes psychological or physical harm to the whistleblower;
- Unfair audit or inspection of the whistleblower's work, as well as the disclosure of the results of such an audit or inspection;
- The cancellation of a license or permit, or any other action that causes administrative disadvantages to the whistleblower.

Source: Korea's Act on the Protection of Public Interest Whistleblowers, Act No. 10472, 29 March 2011, Article 2 (6).

Thailand could consider developing a mechanism to sanction those who retaliate against whistleblowers

It is not enough to establish legislative mechanisms to protect whistleblowers from potential reprisals. To be effective, a whistleblower protection framework should also include penalties for those who retaliate against a whistleblower. In Thailand, there is no legal provision for sanctions for retaliation. When developing a new dedicated whistleblower protection system, PACC could consider introducing sanctions for retaliation in order to deter wrongdoers from intimidating or exercising reprisals against whistleblowers. Such an initiative may also serve to reinforce the message that reprisals against whistleblowers will not be tolerated.

In terms of penalties, the approach to applying penalties varies, even among OECD countries where the whistleblower protection systems are established by a dedicated whistleblower protection law (OECD, 2016[5]). For instance, Australia's whistleblower protection system invokes imprisonment for two years – or 120 penalty units,[1] or both – in case of reprisal against whistleblowers[2]; while in the United States, criminal sanctions are imposed against employers who retaliate against whistleblowers.[3] In Korea, the punishment for retaliation varies depending on the type of reprisal that took place (Box 5.4). Regardless of the approach chosen, specifying a disciplinary course of action for those who take reprisals against whistleblowers can strengthen the robustness of the whistleblower framework and encourage those with information about potential wrongdoing to come forward.

Box 5.4. Sanctions for retaliation in Korea

Under Korea's Protection of Public Interest Whistleblowers Act, anyone whose actions fall into any of the following categories shall be punished by imprisonment for not more than two years or by a fine not exceeding KRW 20 million:

1. A person who implemented disadvantageous measures described in Article 2, Subparagraph 6, Item (a) [removal from office, release from office, dismissal or any other unfavourable personnel action equivalent to the loss of status at work] against a public interest whistleblower.

2. A person who did not carry out the decision to take protective measures confirmed by the Commission or by an administrative proceeding.

In addition, any person whose actions fall into any of the following categories shall be punished by imprisonment for not more than one year or a fine not exceeding KRW 10 million.

1. A person who implemented disadvantageous measures that fall under any of Items (b) through (g) in Article 2, Subparagraph 6 against the public interest whistleblower [(b) disciplinary action, suspension from office, reduction in pay, demotion, restriction on promotion and any other unfair personnel actions; (c) work reassignment, transfer, denial of duties, rearrangement of duties or any other personnel actions that are against the whistleblower's will; (d) discrimination in performance evaluation, peer review, etc. and subsequent discrimination in the payment of wages, bonuses, etc.; (e) cancellation of education, training or other self-development opportunities; restriction or removal of budget, workforce or other available resources, suspension of access to security information or classified information; cancellation of authorisation to handle security information or classified information; or any other discrimination or measure detrimental to the working conditions of the whistleblower; (f) putting the whistleblower's name on a black list, as well as the release of such a blacklist, bullying, the use of violence and abusive language toward the whistleblower, or any other action that causes psychological or physical harm to the whistleblower; (g) unfair audit or inspection of the whistleblower's work as well as the disclosure of the results of such an audit or inspection; (h) cancellation of a license or permit, or any other action that causes administrative disadvantages to the whistleblower].

2. A person who obstructs public interest whistleblowing, etc., or forces a public interest whistleblower to rescind his/her case, etc., in violation of Article 15, Paragraph 2.

Source: Korea's Protection of Public Interest Whistleblowers Act No. 10 472, Chapter V, Articles 30 (2) and (3).

Thailand could consider establishing measures to preclude reporting in bad faith

Discouraging individuals from exploiting the system for personal reasons is also a key element of an effective whistleblower protection framework. Indeed, according to the United Nations Office on Drugs and Crime (UNODC) Technical Guide to the United Nations Convention Against Corruption, "good faith should be presumed in favour of the person claiming protection, but where it is proved that the report was false and not in good faith, there should be appropriate remedies" (UNODC, 2015[7]; UNODC, 2009[8]). Such measures include the removal or forfeiture of protections, such as confidentiality, and in some cases libel and defamation suits, fines or imprisonment.

In Thailand, reporting in bad faith may be subject to a penal code if any damage occurs as a result of such reporting. However, this is not explicitly stated in the Executive Measures in Anti-Corruption Act, B.E. 2551. In developing a dedicated whistleblower protection law, PACC could consider establishing measures to preclude reporting in bad faith. When considering measures to discourage bad-faith reporting, the key element of the offence of slanderous reporting lies not in the falsity of the allegation itself, but in the knowledge, on the day the allegation was made, that it was false. Box 5.5 contains examples from OECD member countries on how to preclude disclosures made in bad faith.

Box 5.5. Measures in place to preclude reporting in bad faith – examples from OECD member countries

A number of OECD countries have measures that remove protection of whistleblowers who disclose in bad faith:

- Korea's Act on the Protection of Public Interest Whistleblowers states that in the event that the public interest whistleblowing was brought forward, if the whistleblower knew or could have known that the information was false, it shall not be deemed a case of public interest whistleblowing.
- In Australia, the protections in the Public Interest Disclosure Act (PID Act)[2] do not apply to those knowingly making a statement that is false or misleading.
- The Anti-Corruption Act in Estonia also removes protections from those who disclose in bad faith. Specifically, it maintains that confidentiality shall not be respected.
- In Hungary, similarly, confidentiality is not ensured in such circumstances, and furthermore, if this bad-faith disclosure has caused unlawful damage or harm to the rights of others, the personal data of the individual who disclosed in bad faith may be disclosed upon request of the person or body entitled to initiate proceedings.
- In Israel, in addition to revoking the protection of individuals who report in bad faith and rendering it a disciplinary matter, an approach comparable to that of Hungary is applied, with respect to the individual who may have been harmed due to a disclosure made in bad faith. Specifically, the Court can render compensation in favour of an employer or another employee if a complaint was filed in bad faith.

Source: (OECD, 2016[5]).

Thailand could consider developing more detailed guidelines for remedies in the event of reprisals

Most whistleblower protection systems include remedies for whistleblowers who have suffered harm. Measures of this nature usually include all direct, indirect and future consequences of reprisal, and can vary from return to employment after unfair termination, job transfers or compensation, or punitive damages in the event that whistleblowers have suffered harm that cannot be remedied by injunctions, such as difficulties in seeking employment or inability to find a new job. Such remedies may take into account not only lost salary but also compensatory damages for pain and suffering (Banisar, 2011[1]).

In Thailand, Section 54 of the Executive Measures in Anti-Corruption Act, B.E. 2551, also makes a reference to remuneration to compensate damage against lives, bodies, health, reputation, properties or any right of the whistleblowers as a consequence of taking action or making statements or passing on information to PACC. However, this provision does not include any details. In drafting a dedicated whistleblower protection law, PACC could further specify such remedies for whistleblowers, to ensure that measures are in place in the event of reprisals.

For example, Canada's Public Servants Disclosure Protection Act (PSDPA) includes a comprehensive list of remedies (Box 5.6). Under UK law, the courts have ruled that compensation can be provided for suffering, based on the system developed under discrimination law (Banisar, 2011[1]). The total amount of damages awarded under the UK Public Interest Disclosure Act (PIDA) in 2009 and 2010 was GBP 2.3 million, the highest award being GBP 800 000 in the case of *John Watkinson v. Royal Cornwall Hospitals NHS Trust* (Public Concern at Work, 2011). The average PIDA award in 2009 and 2010 was GBP 58 000, by comparison with average awards of GBP 18 584, GBP 19 499 and GBP 52 087 in race, sex and disability discrimination cases respectively (Public Concern at Work, 2011).

Box 5.6. Remedies for public sector whistleblowers in Canada

To provide an appropriate remedy to the complainant, the Tribunal may, by order, require the employer or the appropriate chief executive, or any person acting on their behalf, to take all necessary measures to

(a) permit the complainant to return to his or her duties;

(b) reinstate the complainant or pay compensation to the complainant in lieu of reinstatement if, in the Tribunal's opinion, the relationship of trust between the parties cannot be restored;

(c) pay to the complainant compensation in an amount not greater than the amount that, in the Tribunal's opinion, is equivalent to the remuneration that would, but for the reprisal, have been paid to the complainant;

(d) rescind any measure or action, including any disciplinary action, and pay compensation to the complainant in an amount not greater than the amount that, in the Tribunal's opinion, is equivalent to any financial or other penalty imposed on the complainant;

(e) pay to the complainant an amount equal to any expenses and any other financial losses incurred by the complainant as a direct result of the reprisal; or

(f) compensate the complainant, by an amount of not more than CAD 10 000, for any pain and suffering that the complainant experienced as a result of the reprisal.

Source: Canada's Public Servants Disclosure Protection Act of 2005, 21.7 (1).

To ensure clear and robust reporting channels, Thailand could consider clearly identifying in the law both the internal and external reporting options for whistleblowers

Whistleblower protection systems often establish one or more channels through which protected disclosures can be made. These generally include internal disclosures, external disclosure to a designated body, and external disclosures to the public or to the media. A variety of channels need to be available to match the circumstances and allow whistleblowers to choose which channel they trust most to use.

First of all, employees who witness wrongdoing should be able to disclose information internally without fear of reprisal. Unimpeded access, free of reprimand and retribution, can pave the way for an open organisational culture between the discloser and management. This open culture should be established by management and be in force throughout the organisation. Organisations should operate on the premise that employees will come forward to management with disclosures of wrongdoing, and that management will support the individual's justification to disclose, and follow the measures in place to protect them and investigate the allegations appropriately. By being receptive to disclosures, and encouraging this as a method of detection, management can mitigate any damage to its reputation that may result if an employee discloses externally.

According to a recent study (Chokprajakchat and Sumretphol, 2017[9]), almost half of the civil servants in Thailand would not report misconduct, for several reasons. First, they are concerned about the consequences for informers and are not sure whether they will be protected. Second, they are concerned about the misconduct of the management and they are not confident that the commanding officials will take the incidents seriously. In addition, they expressed concerns that the violators might not be punished and that the provisions of the Code are too abstract and not clear enough.

In Thailand, PACC currently acts as a designated agency for external disclosure under the Executive Measures in Anti-Corruption Act, B.E. 2551. PACC is responsible for managing a hotline (#1206) where citizens can report any corruption-related wrongdoing, and citizens can also email the PACC. As for internal disclosure channels, each Ministry has an Anti-Corruption Operation Centre responsible for dealing with any complaints relating to corruption. While these centres could provide relevant information and direct the whistleblowers to PACC, they are not mandated to provide an adequate response within a certain timeframe or to take appropriate action when a whistleblower comes forward. To establish an effective internal disclosure channel, PACC, together with other government agencies, could consider strengthening the capacity of the Anti-Corruption Operation Centres to deal with enquires from internal whistleblowers. Canada offers a good example of an internal reporting mechanism in which senior officers for disclosure promote a positive environment for disclosing wrongdoing and handle disclosures of wrongdoing by public servants within their organisation (Box 5.7).

In developing a dedicated whistleblower protection law, Thailand could consider ensuring alternative channels through which individuals may disclose information. Internal and external options operating concurrently could allow potential whistleblowers to choose where they would like to submit their disclosures.

For example, the UK has a tiered approach permitting disclosures to be made to one of the following tiers of persons: Tier 1 – internal disclosures to employers or Ministers of the Crown; Tier 2 – regulatory disclosures to prescribed bodies (e.g. the Financial Services Authority or Inland Revenue); and Tier 3 – wider disclosures to the police, media, members of Parliament and non-prescribed regulators. Each tier requires an incrementally higher threshold of conditions to satisfy for the whistleblower to be protected. This is intended to encourage internal reporting and for using external reporting channels only as a last resort.

Box 5.7. Internal reporting mechanisms in Canada

As provided under Sections 12 and 13 of the Public Servants Disclosure Protection Act (PSDPA), if public servants have information that could indicate serious wrongdoing, they can bring this matter, in confidence and without fear of reprisal, to the attention of their immediate supervisor, their senior officer for disclosure or the Public Sector Integrity Commissioner. The senior officer for disclosure helps promote a positive environment for disclosing wrongdoing and deals with disclosures of wrongdoing made by public servants within the organisation.

The senior officer's duties and powers within an organisation include the following, in accordance with the internal disclosure procedures established under the PSDPA:

1. Provide information, advice and guidance to public servants regarding the organisation's internal disclosure procedures, including the making of disclosures, the conduct of investigations into disclosures, and the handling of disclosures made to supervisors.
2. Receive and record disclosures, and review them, to establish whether there are sufficient grounds for further action under the PSDPA.
3. Manage investigations into disclosures, including determining whether to deal with a disclosure under the PSDPA, initiate an investigation or cease an investigation.
4. Co-ordinate handling of a disclosure with the senior officer of another federal public sector organisation, if a disclosure or an investigation into a disclosure involves that other organisation.
5. Notify the person(s) who made a disclosure, in writing, of the outcome of any review and/or investigation into the disclosure and on the status of actions taken as a result of the disclosure, as appropriate.
6. Report the findings of investigations, as well as any systemic problems that may give rise to wrongdoing, directly to his or her chief executive, with recommendations for corrective action, if any.

Source: Treasury Board of Canada Secretariat, https://www.canada.ca/en/revenue-agency/corporate/careers-cra/information-moved/code-integrity-professional-conduct-we-work.html.

To support a whistleblower protection system, Thailand could consider promoting a broad communication strategy, increasing awareness of the issue through various channels

An open organisational culture and whistleblower protection legislation should be supported by effective awareness-raising, communication, training and evaluation efforts. Employees and the public need to understand how whistleblowers are important in protecting the public interest by shedding light on misconduct prejudicial to the effective management and delivery of public services and ultimately, the fairness of the whole public service. An organisational culture of openness is vital, since it reinforces most incentives and protection measures for whistleblowers. Awareness-raising activities could for example include the publication of an annual report by a relevant oversight body or authority, including information on the outcome of the cases brought forward; the compensation for whistleblowers and recoveries that resulted from information provided by whistleblowers during the year; as well as the average time it took to process a case.

PACC could consider promoting a broad communication strategy, and increasing awareness efforts through various channels to create favourable social conditions for whistleblower protection. Better awareness of the issue can positively impact the perception and language of whistleblowing and also facilitate implementation of the law.

As part of the UK's awareness-raising activities, the Civil Service Commission includes a statement in staff manuals assuring members of the staff that it is safe to raise concerns (Box 5.8).

Box 5.8. Example of a statement to staff encouraging them to raise concerns

"We encourage everyone who works here to raise any concerns they have. We encourage 'whistleblowing' within the organisation to help us put things right if they are going wrong. If you think something is wrong, please tell us and give us a chance to properly investigate and consider your concerns. We encourage you to raise concerns and will ensure that you do not suffer a detriment for doing so."

Source: UK's Civil Service Commission: http://civilservicecommission.independent.gov.uk/wp-content/uploads/2014/02/Whistleblowing-and-the-Civil-Service-Code.pdf.

Comprehensive awareness-raising campaigns will counter any perception that blowing the whistle shows a lack of loyalty to the organisation. Well-targeted campaigns make clear that civil servants' loyalty belongs first and foremost to the public interest, and not to their managers. In other words, increasing the awareness of whistleblowing and whistleblower protection not only enhances understanding of these mechanisms, but is an important mechanism for improving the often negative cultural connotations linked to the term "whistleblower". Communicating the importance of whistleblowing from, for example, a public health and safety perspective can help improve the public view of whistleblowers as important safeguards of public interest, rather than as informants reporting on their colleagues (Box 5.9).

Box 5.9. 'Courage when it counts'

In 2013, the campaign "Courage when it counts" was launched by the Advice Centre in the Netherlands. The idea behind the initiative was to portray whistleblowers as vulnerable heroes who put their fears aside to come forward with disclosures of wrongdoing. As part of this campaign, a series of photographs of employees with the courage to speak out were put on display. The aim of these visual representations was to provide an alternative image to that of ringing bells, which usually frame reports on whistleblowers in the Netherlands.

Source: Advice Centre for Whistleblowers in the Netherlands (2013), Annual Report, www.adviespuntklokkenluiders.nl/wp-content/uploads/2015/03/advice-centre-for-whistleblowers-in-the-netherlands-annual-report-2013.pdf.

Reviewing existing whistleblower protection legislation can help evaluate its purpose and effectiveness

To ensure that the mechanisms in place fulfill the purposes for which they were introduced, countries should regularly review their whistleblower protection systems and the effectiveness of their implementation. If necessary, the legislation on which they are based can be amended to reflect the findings. Provisions regarding the review of effectiveness, enforcement and impact of whistleblower protection laws have been introduced by a number of OECD countries, including Australia, Canada, Japan and the Netherlands. Japan's whistleblower protection act specifically outlines that the Government must take the necessary measures, based on the findings of the review.

Once Thailand establishes a dedicated whistleblower protection law, PACC could start collecting data on the legislation, to evaluate its purpose, implementation and effectiveness. This can include information on i) the number of cases received; ii) the outcomes of cases (i.e. if the case was dismissed, accepted, investigated and validated); iii) compensation for whistleblowers and recoveries that resulted from information from whistleblowers; iv) awareness of whistleblower mechanisms; and v) the time it takes to process cases. This data, in particular information on the outcome of cases, can be used in the review of a country's legislation, to assess whether the framework is working effectively to protect whistleblowers in practice. Surveys can also be distributed among staff to review their awareness, trust and confidence in these mechanisms.

Proposals for action

- Thailand could consider developing a dedicated law to protect whistleblowers in the public and private sectors, in addition to existing witness-protection arrangements. PACC could be the institution responsible for implementing a new whistleblower protection law.
- In developing a dedicated law, Thailand could consider establishing a clear definition for whistleblowers of the types of wrongdoing that justify coverage under the whistleblower protection system, a comprehensive overview of the types of retaliation against whistleblowers, a mechanism to sanction those who retaliate against whistleblowers, measures to preclude reporting in bad faith, and the different types of remedies available to whistleblowers.
- Thailand could consider clearly identifying in the law the reporting options for whistleblowers, from internal to external. In this respect, the PACC and other government agencies could consider increasing the capacity of the Anti-Corruption Operation Centres to deal with enquiries from potential whistleblowers.
- Thailand could consider promoting a broad communication strategy and undertaking increased awareness efforts through various channels. PACC, together with NACC and other government agencies, could consider developing a broad communication strategy and initiating public information campaigns to create favourable social conditions for introducing a whistleblower protection mechanism.
- Once a dedicated law to protect whistleblowers is in place, Thailand could start collecting data on the application of the whistleblower protection legislation to evaluate its purpose, implementation and effectiveness. PACC could be the lead agency for this task.

Notes

[1] In Australia, penalty units are used to describe the fines payable under Commonwealth laws. By multiplying the AUS equivalent of one penalty unit, the fine for an offence is set.

[2] Australia's Public Interest Disclosure Act, Subdivision B, Part 2 – Section 19.

[3] The US Federal Criminal Code 18 U.S.C. §1513 (e) states that "whoever knowingly, with the intent to retaliate, takes any action harmful to any person, including interference with the lawful employment or livelihood of any person, for providing to a law enforcement officer any truthful information relating to the commission or possible commission of any Federal offense, shall be fined under this title or imprisoned not more than 10 years, or both."

References

Banisar, D. (2011), "Whistleblowing: International Standards and Developments", in *Corruption and Transparency: Debating the Frontiers between State, Market and Society*, I. Sandoval, ed., World Bank-Institute for Social Research, UNAM, Washington, D.C, https://papers.ssrn.com/sol3/papers.cfm?abstract_id=1753180. [1]

Chokprajakchat, S. and N. Sumretphol (2017), "Implementation of the code of professional ethics for Thai civil servants", *Kasetsart Journal of Social Sciences*, Vol. 38, pp. 129-135, http://dx.doi.org/10.1016/j.kjss.2016.03.004. [9]

Latimer, P. and A. Brown (2008), "Whistleblower Laws: International Best Practice", *SSRN Electronic Journal*, http://dx.doi.org/10.2139/ssrn.1326766. [3]

OECD (2014), *OECD Survey on Managing Conflict of Interest in the Executive Branch and Whistleblower Protection*, http://www.oecd.org/gov/ethics/2014-survey-managing-conflict-of-interest.pdf. [6]

OECD (2016), *Committing to Effective Whistleblower Protection*, OECD Publishing, Paris, http://dx.doi.org/10.1787/9789264252639-en. [5]

Transparency International (2009), *Alternative to silence: Whistleblower protection in 10 European countries*, https://www.transparency.org/whatwedo/publication/alternative_to_silence_whistleblower_protection_in_10_european_countries. [2]

Transparency International (2013), *Whistleblower Protection and the UN Convention Against Corruption*, http://www.europarl.europa.eu/meetdocs/2009_2014/documents/libe/dv/ti_report_/ti_report_en.pdf (accessed on 14 February 2018). [4]

UNODC (2009), *Technical Guide to the United Nations Convention Against Corruption*, http://www.unodc.org/documents/corruption/Technical_Guide_UNCAC.pdf. [8]

UNODC (2015), *Resource Guide on Good Practices in the Protection of Reporting Persons*, http://www.unodc.org/documents/corruption/Publications/2015/15-04741_Person_Guide_eBook.pdf (accessed on 14 February 2018). [7]

ORGANISATION FOR ECONOMIC CO-OPERATION AND DEVELOPMENT

The OECD is a unique forum where governments work together to address the economic, social and environmental challenges of globalisation. The OECD is also at the forefront of efforts to understand and to help governments respond to new developments and concerns, such as corporate governance, the information economy and the challenges of an ageing population. The Organisation provides a setting where governments can compare policy experiences, seek answers to common problems, identify good practice and work to co-ordinate domestic and international policies.

The OECD member countries are: Australia, Austria, Belgium, Canada, Chile, the Czech Republic, Denmark, Estonia, Finland, France, Germany, Greece, Hungary, Iceland, Ireland, Israel, Italy, Japan, Korea, Latvia, Luxembourg, Mexico, the Netherlands, New Zealand, Norway, Poland, Portugal, the Slovak Republic, Slovenia, Spain, Sweden, Switzerland, Turkey, the United Kingdom and the United States. The European Union takes part in the work of the OECD.

OECD Publishing disseminates widely the results of the Organisation's statistics gathering and research on economic, social and environmental issues, as well as the conventions, guidelines and standards agreed by its members.

OECD PUBLISHING, 2, rue André-Pascal, 75775 PARIS CEDEX 16
(04 2018 03 1 P) ISBN 978-92-64-29191-1 – 2018

www.ingramcontent.com/pod-product-compliance
Lightning Source LLC
LaVergne TN
LVHW081412110826
845149LV00010B/1720
* 9 7 8 9 2 6 4 2 9 1 9 1 1 *